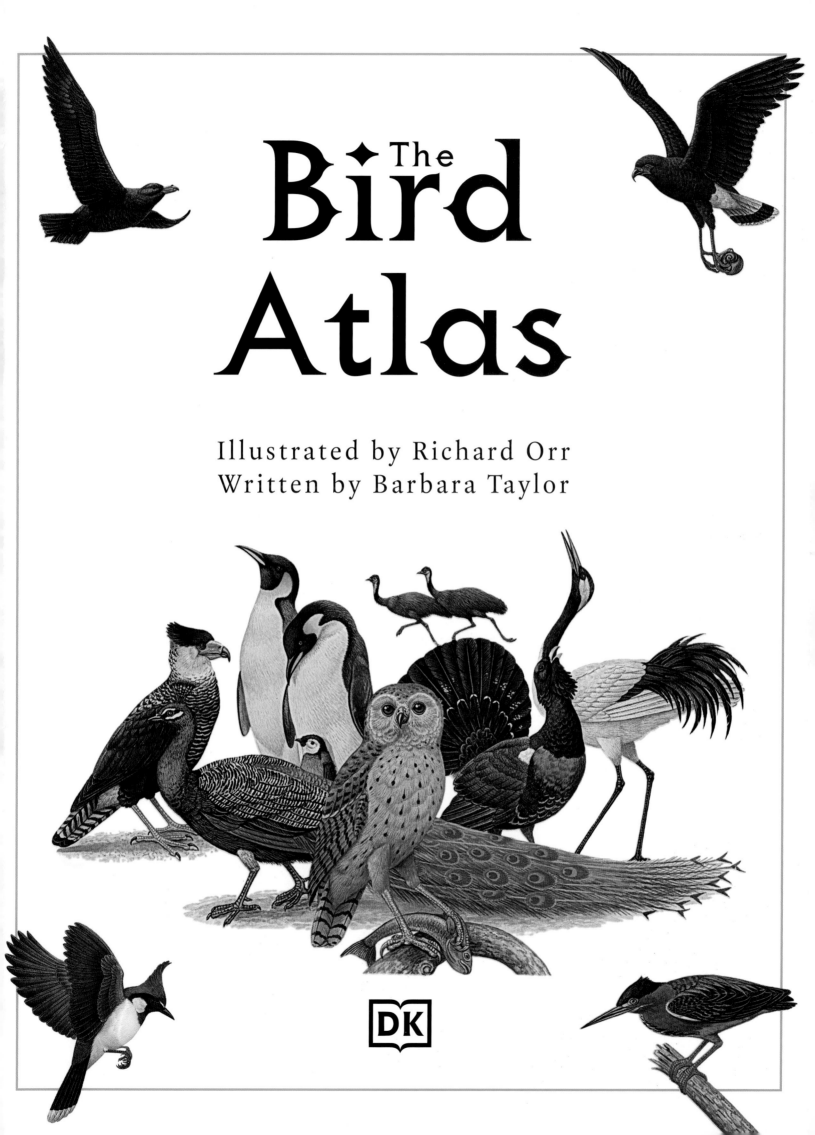

The Bird Atlas

Illustrated by Richard Orr
Written by Barbara Taylor

DK

DK | Penguin Random House

REVISED EDITION
Senior Art Editor Shreya Anand
Editor Ben Ffrancon Davies
Assistant Editor Manjari Thakur
US Editor Megan Douglass **US Executive Editor** Lori Cates Hand
Managing Editors Christine Stroyan, Kingshuk Ghoshal
Managing Art Editors Anna Hall, Govind Mittal
Senior Picture Researcher Surya Sankash Sarangi
Production Editor Kavita Varma
Senior Production Controller Jude Crozier
DTP Designer Bimlesh Tiwary **Jacket Designer** Akiko Kato
Jacket Design Development Manager Sophia MTT
Publisher Andrew Macintyre **Art Director** Karen Self
Publishing Director Jonathan Metcalf
Consultant Derek Harvey

FIRST EDITION
Project Editor Anderley Moore **Art Editor** Sheilagh Noble
Designer Heather Blackham **Production** Shelagh Gibson
Managing Editor Susan Peach **Managing Art Editor** Jacquie Gulliver
Bird Consultant Michael Chinery

This American Edition, 2021
First American Edition, 1993
Published in the United States by DK Publishing
1450 Broadway, Suite 801, New York, NY 10018

Copyright © 1993, 2021 Dorling Kindersley Limited
DK, a Division of Penguin Random House LLC
21 22 23 24 25 10 9 8 7 6 5 4 3 2 1
001–316677–Jan/2021

A catalog record for this book is available from the Library of Congress.
ISBN 978-0-7440-2735-8

DK books are available at special discounts when purchased
in bulk for sales promotions, premiums, fund-raising, or educational use.
For details, contact: DK Publishing Special Markets,
1450 Broadway, Suite 801, New York, NY 10018
SpecialSales@dk.com

Printed and bound in Malaysia

For the curious
www.dk.com

MIX
Paper from
responsible sources
FSC™ C018179

This book was made with
Forest Stewardship Council ™
certified paper—one small step in DK's
commitment to a sustainable future.
For more information go to
www.dk.com/our-green-pledge

CONTENTS

How to Use This Atlas

THE BIRD ATLAS IS ARRANGED in order of continent—the Americas, Europe, Africa, Asia, Australasia, and Antarctica. A double-page, such as the one on Africa (right), introduces the continent as a whole. This is followed by pages showing the main places where birds live—their habitats—within that continent.

On any page you can see which continent it is about by looking at the heading in the top left-hand corner; the habitat featured is given in the top right-hand corner. The sample pages here show how the information is presented on the two main types of pages—continental and habitat pages—and explain the maps, symbols, and abbreviations used.

Continental pages

These pages introduce the continent and give an overview of the climate, landscape, main bird habitats, typical birds, and amazing birds to be found there. A large map shows the size of the continent, its position on the globe, and major geographical features. There is usually a feature showing how the position of the continent has changed over millions of years.

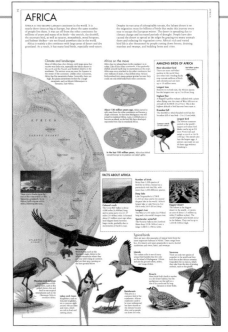

Where on Earth?

The red shaded area on this globe shows the location of the habitat featured on the page. The shaded area on this globe shows the position of Central America and the Caribbean within the Americas.

Bird symbols

Symbols of each of the birds illustrated on the page show the main areas where each species lives, although some birds live all over the region. By looking at the key, you can identify the birds and then find them on the map.

How big?

Length: 1 ft 4 in (40 cm)

Labels next to each bird tell you how big it is, from the tip of the bill to the end of the tail. Sometimes male and female birds are very different in size. In these cases, measurements for males and females are given separately. In some cases, the wingspan, length of tail feathers, or height of the bird are also given. For example, on this page you can find out the length of the male quetzal's remarkable tail feathers.

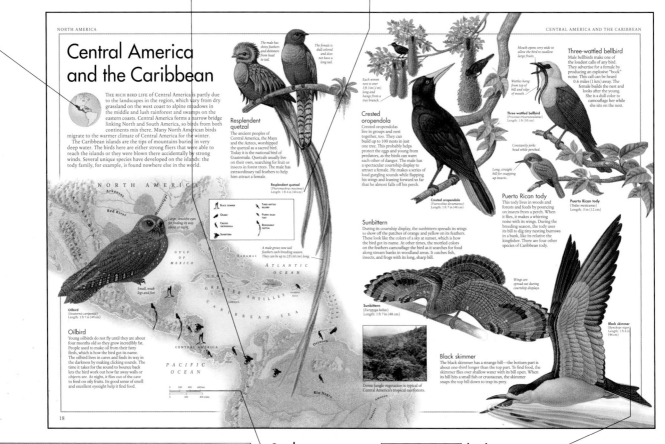

Scale

You can use this scale to figure out the size of the area shown on the map.

Latin names

Black skimmer
(*Rynchops niger*)

Scientists have given each bird species a Latin name. This means that everyone can use the same name to identify birds, no matter what language they speak. A bird's Latin name is divided into two parts. The first is a group name given to a number of similar birds. For example, *Rynchops* is the group name for skimmers. The second part identifies the particular species of bird and often tells you something more specific about it. In this case *niger*, the Latin word for "black."

ABBREVIATIONS USED IN THE ATLAS:

Metric		Imperial	
mm	millimeter	in	inch
cm	centimeter	ft	foot
m	meter	mph	miles per hour
km	kilometer	sq miles	square miles
sq km	square kilometers	lb	pound
kph	kilometers per hour	°F	fahrenheit
kg	kilogram		
°C	celsius		

What Is a Bird?

BIRDS ARE THE ONLY LIVING ANIMALS in the world that have feathers. They also lay eggs, breathe air, and are warm-blooded, meaning that they keep their body temperature the same at all times. Birds evolved from reptiles about 150 million years ago. The earliest bird we know of, *Archaeopteryx* (meaning "ancient wing"), lived at this time. It was about the size of a crow and had feathers, although it probably couldn't fly very well. The 10,964 or so species of bird alive today have developed from early birds like *Archaeopteryx*.

Archaeopteryx

Body or contour feather from a red lory.

Down feather from a pigeon.

Flight feather from a Guinea fowl.

Feathers

A bird has a huge number of feathers. Even a small bird, such as a wren, has more than 1,000 feathers. There are three main types of feather— flight feathers on the wings and tail, body feathers which give a bird its shape, and fluffy down feathers to keep it warm. Flight feathers are made of strands called barbs which hook together. If the hooks come apart, they can be drawn together again, like zipping up a zipper. Each year, a bird sheds or molts most of its feathers and grows new ones to replace them.

A bird's wing is light, strong, and flexible so it will not snap as the bird twists and turns through the air.

Peregrine falcon
(Falco peregrinus)

The bill is lightweight, but very strong.

Bird bones

A bird has a bony skeleton inside its body to support and protect its delicate organs. But the whole skeleton of flying birds is very light and the long bones in their wings and legs are hollow, with a honeycomb of stiff supporting struts (above). This means they have less weight to lift off the ground and stay up in the air.

A bird uses its tail feathers for steering as it flies through the air.

Pigeon
(Columba livia)

Pigeons and many other birds have a flapping flight. Others, such as eagles and albatrosses, glide long distances. Hummingbirds can even hover.

Birds have scaly legs like their reptile ancestors.

How birds fly

Birds are the largest, fastest, and most powerful flying animals alive. Their smooth, streamlined shape lets them cut through the air easily, while their powerful chest muscles flap their wings, pushing them along. A bird's wings are curved on top and flat underneath. As a bird flies, this airfoil shape creates an area of high air pressure under the wing and an area of low air pressure above it. The high pressure under the wing pushes the bird up into the air. Some birds, such as penguins and ostriches, cannot fly—they run or swim very fast instead.

BIRD BILLS

Birds use their bills to catch and hold their food, care for their feathers, and build nests. The size and shape of a bird's bill depends on what it eats and where it finds its food.

Pine grosbeak
(Pinicola enucleator)
Seed-eater

White-cheeked barbet
(Megalaima viridis)
Fruit- and insect-eater

African paradise flycatcher
(Terpsiphone viridis)
Insect-eater

Australian darter
(Anhinga novaehollandiae)
Fish-eater

Eggs and chicks

All birds lay eggs. The eggshell is hard to protect the developing chick, but air can still pass through. The chick also has a food store inside the egg. While the chick develops, the parents have to keep the eggs warm by sitting on them. This is called incubation. Many birds are blind, featherless, and helpless when they hatch. Other birds, such as this duckling, spend longer inside the egg and so are better developed when they hatch. They can run around and fend for themselves almost as soon as they hatch.

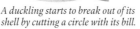

A duckling starts to break out of its shell by cutting a circle with its bill.

When the young bird pushes itself out of the shell its feathers are still wet.

Within three hours its feathers are dry and fluffy and it can run around.

Where Birds Live

Birds live in every corner of the globe. They have spread so far because they can fly from one place to another, live on a variety of foods, and maintain a constant body temperature in most types of weather.

The place where a bird lives is called its habitat. This is rather like its "home address." A bird's habitat must provide food, shelter, and somewhere to nest. Some birds, such as the barn owl, can live in a range of habitats from woodland to scrub; others are more specialized (toucans, for example, live only in the rainforests of Central and South America). Some birds stay permanently in one habitat, while others move away—migrate—at certain times of year. There are an increasing number of human-made habitats, such as houses, parks, and backyards. Some of the most common birds, such as starlings and sparrows, have adapted to live in these new habitats near people.

The main types of bird habitat around the world are shown at the bottom of these pages.

Look-alikes

Birds that live in similar habitats or feed on similar things have often evolved to look similar. The map shows the world's grasslands and three related birds that live in these habitats in different parts of the world: the rhea, ostrich, and emu. Each is flightless, but has evolved strong running legs to escape danger. Sometimes birds can end up looking similar, even though they are not related. This is called convergent evolution. For example, hummingbirds from America and honeyeaters from Australasia probe flowers for nectar, but belong to completely different groups of the bird family tree.

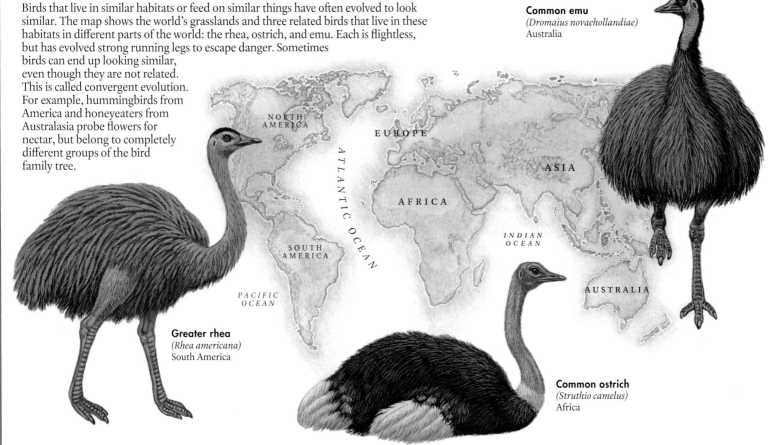

Common emu
(Dromaius novaehollandiae)
Australia

Greater rhea
(Rhea americana)
South America

Common ostrich
(Struthio camelus)
Africa

NORTH AMERICA · EUROPE · ASIA · AFRICA · ATLANTIC OCEAN · SOUTH AMERICA · PACIFIC OCEAN · INDIAN OCEAN · AUSTRALIA

 ### Polar and tundra
The Arctic in the north and the Antarctic in the south are among the harshest environments on Earth. Freezing temperatures, howling gales, and long dark winters mean that few birds can live there, but seabirds nest along the coasts in summer. Surrounding the Arctic is a cold, treeless region called the tundra. In summer, birds such as waders, ducks, and geese flock there to raise their young as there are few predators, and plenty of food and light.

Find out more: pages 8–9, 58–59

 ### Taiga
Coniferous trees such as pine, fir, and spruce grow in a huge forest called the taiga, which stretches across the top of North America, Europe, and Asia. The taiga is one of the largest forest areas in the world. Most coniferous trees have needlelike leaves that stay on the trees all year. Birds feed on the tree cones and help spread the tree seeds. Summers are usually mild, but winters are bitterly cold. Many birds fly south to warmer places in winter.

Find out more: pages 12–13, 28–29

 ### Temperate deciduous woodlands
Deciduous, or broad-leaved, woodlands grow south of the dark conifer woods. Many of the trees, such as oak and beech, lose their leaves in winter, but there is plenty of rainfall all year, and the climate is generally mild. These woodlands provide plenty of food and nesting places for birds in spring and summer.

Find out more: pages 12–13, 52–53

 ### Grasslands
Grasslands occur where the climate is too dry and the soil is too poor for most trees to survive. Fires are common in this habitat, but the grasses grow back. Grasslands provide plenty of food for seed- and insect-eating birds. Tropical grasslands, such as the African savanna, are hot all year with long dry spells. Temperate grasslands, such as the South American pampas, are cooler, with hot summers and long, cold winters.

Find out more: pages 23, 38–39

ISLAND EVOLUTION

Many rare and unusual birds live on islands, such as the Hawaiian Islands (shown below), the Galápagos Islands, Madagascar, and New Zealand. These species have developed in unique ways because they have been cut off from their relatives on the mainland for a long time. For example, on the Hawaiian Islands, a finch-like bird arrived some 5–6 million years ago. Since there were few other birds to compete with it, this bird evolved into around 40 different species called honeycreepers.

Mountain habitats

Mountains such as the Himalayas in Asia (right), the Andes in South America, the Rocky Mountains in North America, and the Alps in Europe provide a wide range of bird habitats. The lower slopes have warm forests, but these merge into grasslands and tundra higher up. Above a certain height—called the tree line—there are no trees because it is too cold for them to grow. Near the very top, the ground is covered with snow and ice, and no birds can live there. Mountain birds have to cope with freezing temperatures, fierce winds, and thin air. Some birds move up and down the mountains with the seasons.

Living together

In any one habitat, different species of bird live side by side. In a rich habitat, such as a deciduous woodland, various kinds of birds can live on a single tree by feeding and nesting at different levels and eating different types of food. Some eat insects, while others prefer seeds. In this way, the birds share the resources of the habitat and are more likely to survive than if they compete with each other for the same things.

Near the top of the tree, tiny birds such as blue tits and wood warblers hang from the smaller twigs and pick insects off the leaves and bark.

In the middle of the tree, birds such as spotted flycatchers dart out from a perch to catch flying insects. Woodpeckers chisel into trunks and branches to find insects. They also dig out nesting holes in the trunk.

On the woodland floor, bigger birds such as the woodcock feed and nest. These birds are usually well camouflaged among the dead leaves. Wrens and other small insect-eaters hop nimbly through the dense thickets of leaves and twigs, where they are hidden from predators.

Wood warbler
(*Phylloscopus sibilatrix*)

Eurasian blue tit
(*Cyanistes caeruleus*)

Great spotted woodpecker
(*Dendrocopus major*)

Spotted flycatcher
(*Muscicapa striata*)

Eurasian woodcock
(*Scolopax rusticola*)

Northern wren
(*Troglodytes troglodytes*)

Scrublands

This warm, dry, dusty habitat with tough shrubs and small trees is found mainly around the shores of the Mediterranean Sea, California in the US, and parts of Australia, where it is called the outback or the bush. Many birds move, or migrate, to these scrublands during the long, hot summers, when there are plenty of insects and seeds to feed on. Some fly away for the cooler, wetter winter months.

Find out more: pages 30–31, 52–53

Deserts

Deserts cover about one-fifth of the Earth's land surface. They are a difficult habitat for birds because there is little rainfall and daytime temperatures are very high. Birds have to rest in the shade during the hottest times of the day and either get water from their food or fly long distances to find it. Important deserts of the world include the western deserts of North America; the Sahara, Kalahari, and Namib deserts in Africa; and the Australian deserts.

Find out more: pages 15, 52–53

Rainforests

Rainforests grow near the equator where it is hot and wet all year. They cover less than 10 percent of the Earth's surface but are home to more than half of all the different species of wildlife living on Earth. Many birds live high up in the treetops, where there is more sunlight, warmth, and food. But birds live at all levels in the forest, sharing the food and space of this rich habitat. The largest birds live on the forest floor.

Find out more: pages 20–21, 36–37, 54–55

Wetlands

Watery environments are a favorite habitat for birds. Herons, ducks, geese, and swans flock to wetlands because there are plenty of fish, insects, and water plants for them to eat, as well as reeds and riverbanks for them to nest in. Trees grow in swampy areas, but there are hardly any trees on marshland. Drainage and pollution of their wetland habitats by people is a major threat to many of these birds.

Find out more: pages 16–17, 40–41

The Arctic

THE ARCTIC REGION lies right at the top of the planet. It is mostly made up of an ice-covered ocean, but it also includes the northern tips of North America, Europe, Asia, and Greenland. Arctic land that is not covered in ice has a low, flat tundra landscape, with many lichens, mosses, grasses, and ground-hugging bushes.

Not many birds can live in the Arctic all year because it is so cold, particularly in winter when it is dark all day from October until March. During the few light summer months, many birds migrate to the Arctic to nest and feed. At this time of year, microscopic plants and animals in the sea grow quickly with the light and warmth. They are eaten by fish, which in turn provide food for millions of gulls, auks, and terns. On the tundra lands, some of the ice melts, flowers make seeds, and insects hatch. Waders, ducks, geese, and smaller birds hurry to eat the seeds or insects, lay their eggs, and raise their young before flying south to escape the harsh Arctic winter.

Snowy owl

Like a silent, white ghost, the snowy owl glides over the Arctic tundra, hunting for birds and small mammals, such as lemmings and hares. When there is plenty of food around, these powerful owls lay lots of eggs because their chicks have a good chance of survival, but when food is scarce, they may not bother to lay any eggs at all.

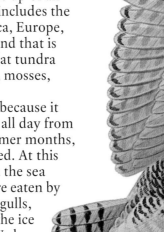

Snowy owl
(*Bubo scandiacus*)
Length: 2 ft 2 in (66 cm)

The female, shown here, is larger than the male and has more black markings.

Food is carried in a pouch or crop. This makes the throat bulge out.

Snowy owls have powerful legs and talons for attacking and carrying off heavy prey.

The male's summer breeding plumage helps him attract a female. He becomes much paler than this in winter.

Lapland longspur

In the summer months, the lapland longspur migrates to the Arctic tundra to nest. There are no trees in the tundra for the male to perch on while he sings to attract females or warn off rival males. Instead, he has to stand on rocks or fly up in the air to sing. The lapland longspur often nests in small groups for protection from predators.

Lapland longspur
(*Calcarius lapponicus*)
Length: 7 in (17 cm)

Little auk

These tiny birds look like the penguins of the Antarctic because they live and feed in a similar way. Their bodies are streamlined for swimming underwater and they use their flipper-like wings to push them along. A thick layer of fat keeps them warm in the cold Arctic seas. Millions of little auks, or dovekies as they are sometimes called, raise their young on the Arctic coasts in summer. They move south in winter, but they do not usually go far beyond the Arctic Circle.

Little auk
(*Alle alle*)
Length: 8 in (20 cm)

Long-tailed duck

In the Arctic summer, the yodeling courtship call of male long-tailed ducks carries long distances across the open tundra landscape. Long-tailed ducks are very good at diving and can plunge as deep as 180 ft (55 m) to chase and catch fish. In areas of shallow water, they take shellfish and other small animals from the muddy bottom.

The female has dark cheek patches.

The male has long tail feathers.

Long-tailed duck
(*Clangula hyemalis*)
Length: 2 ft (60 cm)

Male and female ducks in summer plumage, which is mainly brown with white patches. In winter, it is the opposite— mainly white with brown patches.

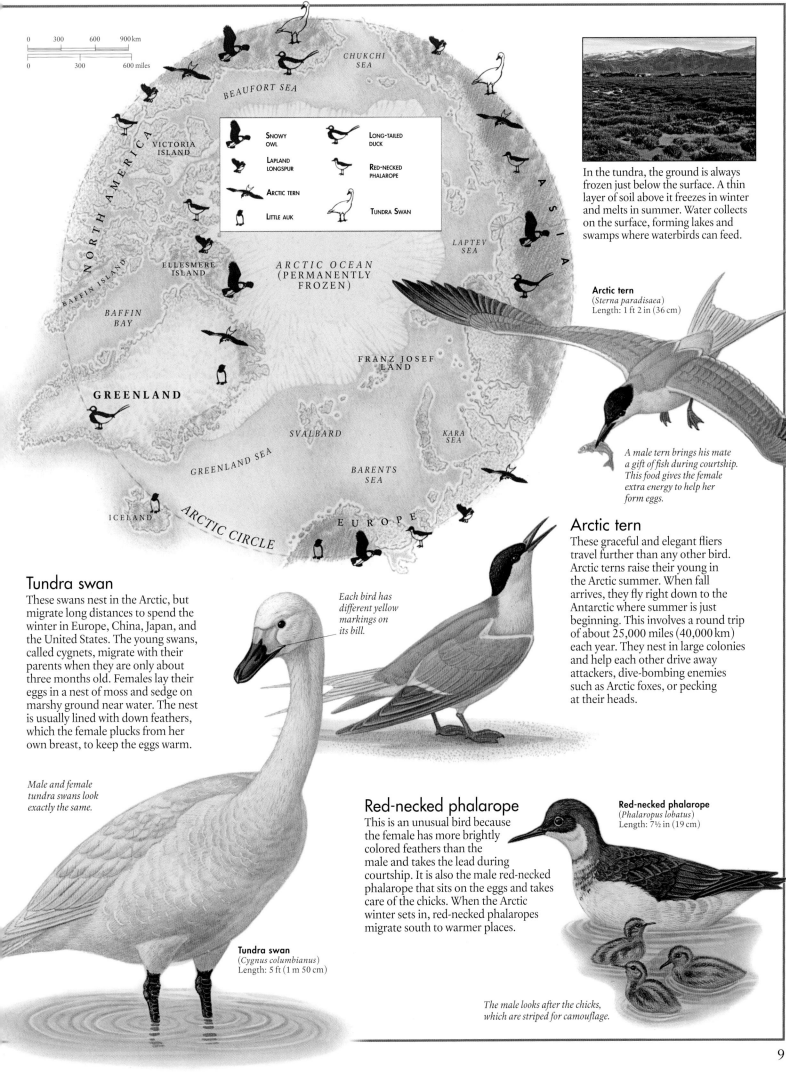

Key (map legend):
- Snowy owl
- Lapland longspur
- Arctic tern
- Little auk
- Long-tailed duck
- Red-necked phalarope
- Tundra Swan

0 300 600 900 km
0 300 600 miles

BEAUFORT SEA
CHUKCHI SEA
NORTH AMERICA
VICTORIA ISLAND
ELLESMERE ISLAND
BAFFIN ISLAND
BAFFIN BAY
GREENLAND
ARCTIC OCEAN (PERMANENTLY FROZEN)
LAPTEV SEA
ASIA
FRANZ JOSEF LAND
KARA SEA
SVALBARD
GREENLAND SEA
BARENTS SEA
ICELAND
ARCTIC CIRCLE
EUROPE

In the tundra, the ground is always frozen just below the surface. A thin layer of soil above it freezes in winter and melts in summer. Water collects on the surface, forming lakes and swamps where waterbirds can feed.

Arctic tern
(*Sterna paradisaea*)
Length: 1 ft 2 in (36 cm)

A male tern brings his mate a gift of fish during courtship. This food gives the female extra energy to help her form eggs.

Arctic tern

These graceful and elegant fliers travel further than any other bird. Arctic terns raise their young in the Arctic summer. When fall arrives, they fly right down to the Antarctic where summer is just beginning. This involves a round trip of about 25,000 miles (40,000 km) each year. They nest in large colonies and help each other drive away attackers, dive-bombing enemies such as Arctic foxes, or pecking at their heads.

Tundra swan

These swans nest in the Arctic, but migrate long distances to spend the winter in Europe, China, Japan, and the United States. The young swans, called cygnets, migrate with their parents when they are only about three months old. Females lay their eggs in a nest of moss and sedge on marshy ground near water. The nest is usually lined with down feathers, which the female plucks from her own breast, to keep the eggs warm.

Each bird has different yellow markings on its bill.

Male and female tundra swans look exactly the same.

Tundra swan
(*Cygnus columbianus*)
Length: 5 ft (1 m 50 cm)

Red-necked phalarope

This is an unusual bird because the female has more brightly colored feathers than the male and takes the lead during courtship. It is also the male red-necked phalarope that sits on the eggs and takes care of the chicks. When the Arctic winter sets in, red-necked phalaropes migrate south to warmer places.

Red-necked phalarope
(*Phalaropus lobatus*)
Length: 7½ in (19 cm)

The male looks after the chicks, which are striped for camouflage.

THE AMERICAS

THE AMERICAS ARE MADE UP of two continents—North America and South America. North America includes the Caribbean islands and Central America, the narrow strip of mountainous land that links the two continents.

South America is generally warmer than North America and contains the greatest variety of bird species on Earth. It was cut off from the other continents for millions of years and many of its birds, such as the hoatzin, the oilbird, rheas, and trumpeters are found nowhere else.

Almost half the world's bird species either breed in the tropical rainforests of South America or visit them on migration.

By contrast, North America has fewer unique species and its bird life is less varied. One reason for this is the large number of cities and farms in the region, but the colder climate is also important. There is less food and shelter available and many birds have to migrate to Central and South America during cold seasons. Also, the last Ice Age wiped out many North American birds or drove them south.

Continents on the move

The Earth's thin surface layer, or crust, is made up of several gigantic pieces called plates, which float on a much thicker layer of liquid rock underneath them. Powerful forces within the Earth move the plates extremely slowly around the globe, carrying the continents with them. This movement is known as continental drift. The continents of North and South America have not always been in the position they are in today. Over millions of years, continental drift has pulled the two continents apart and pushed them together again, altering their shape and landscape.

About 200 million years ago
all the continents were joined together in one landmass known as Pangaea, but this was slowly beginning to break apart.

About 50 million years ago
North America had separated from Europe and Asia, and South America was an island on its own. Many unique and unusual birds evolved in South America because the birds could not mix with those in other continents.

About 3 million years ago
the continents had moved into roughly their current positions. South America had joined up with North America. Birds could use the land bridge of Central America to move north and south between the two continents.

Climate and landscape

The Americas stretch from the Arctic in the north almost down to Antarctica in the south. All the major types of habitat in the world can be found there, including dark evergreen forests, sunny broad-leaved woodlands, dry grasslands, humid rainforests, deserts, and swamps. Two huge mountain ranges—the Rockies and the Andes—stretch down the western side of the region and stop some birds moving freely from east to west.

Heavy storms occur in the Caribbean Sea in late summer. They can blow birds migrating from North America off course.

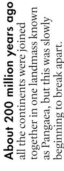

Bee hummingbird
(*Mellisuga helenae*)

AMAZING BIRDS OF THE AMERICAS

Tiniest bird
The bee hummingbird is the smallest bird in the world. An adult male is only 2.2 in (5.7 cm) long.

Slowest flight
The American woodcock flies incredibly slowly for a bird at only 5 mph (8 kph).

Fastest spread
In 1890, 120 starlings were introduced to New York. In only 60 years, they had spread across most of North America.

Heaviest nest
The bald eagle builds the largest nest of any bird. A single nest can weigh 4,400 lb (2,000 kg), about the same as two army jeeps.

Deepest dive
The thick-billed murre, or Brünnich's guillemot, dives up to 690 ft (210 m).

Quickest runner
The greater roadrunner is the fastest-running flying bird. It runs up to 18 mph (29 kph).

Greater roadrunner
(*Geococcyx californianus*)

Millions of pelicans and other seabirds nest off the west coast of South America. People collect their droppings (guano) for fertilizer.

CENTRAL AMERICA

CARIBBEAN SEA

ANDES

Amazon

SOUTH AMERICA

PAMPAS

ATLANTIC OCEAN

ANDES

PACIFIC OCEAN

Rainforests
There are nearly 40 species of toucan, toucanet, and aracari living only in South American rainforests. This toco toucan is a common species.

Woodlands
Crows, magpies, and jays, such as this noisy blue jay, are common in the woods of North America. More than 30 species of jay live in the Americas.

Rivers, lakes, and swamps
Perching ducks, such as this wood duck, nest in tree holes near water. Other typical ducks of the Americas include whistling ducks, steamer ducks, teal, eider, and scoter.

Mountains
Guans, such as this shy Andean guan, live mainly in the mountain forests of South America.

Grasslands
This burrowing owl lives on the grasslands and deserts of the Americas. Nearly 60 species of owl live in the Americas, including screech owls and pygmy owls.

Deserts
All the wrens in the world except for one species live in the Americas. This cactus wren prefers a desert habitat.

FACTS ABOUT THE AMERICAS

Number of birds
More than 3,400 species of bird live in South America. Colombia alone has more than 1,800 breeding species. Fewer than 1,000 species of bird are found in North America north of Mexico.

Longest mountains
The Andes are the longest mountain chain on Earth, stretching for more than 4,500 miles (7,250 km) down the west side of South America.

Long river
The Amazon in South America is the second longest river in the world, after the Nile. One-fifth of all the fresh water on Earth flows through it each day. The river pours into the Atlantic Ocean with such force that it is possible to scoop up a glass of fresh water 200 miles (320 km) out to sea.

Largest lake
Lake Superior is the largest of the Great Lakes of North America and the largest freshwater lake in the world.

Highest temperature
Death Valley in North America is one of the hottest places on Earth. Summer temperatures are often higher than 131°F (55°C).

Oldest mountains
The Appalachians are some of the oldest mountains in the world and were formed more than 250 million years ago.

Highest waterfall
The Angel Falls in Venezuela are the highest in the world at 3,212 ft (979 m).

Typical birds
Here are just a few examples of typical birds from the most important habitats of the Americas. You can find out more about them on the next few pages.

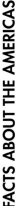

Forests and Woodlands

A HUGE EXPANSE OF evergreen forest stretches right across Canada, in a broad belt up to 500 miles (800 km) wide. It is sometimes called the boreal forest—after Boreas, the Greek god of the North Wind. The cones, buds, and needles of conifer trees provide food for a variety of birds, such as grosbeaks, juncos, and crossbills. But the weather is bitterly cold in winter, and many birds fly south to escape the harsh climate.

To the south of these dark forests are areas of woodland where the climate is warmer and moister. The most common trees are broad-leaved species, such as oak, maple, walnut, and hickory, which lose their leaves in winter. The carpet of decaying leaves is full of insects that birds can feed on. There is also a greater variety of nesting places in these sunlit woodlands than in the dark conifer forests further north.

Bald eagle

The national bird of the United States, the bald eagle has a spectacular courtship display. A male and a female bird lock talons and somersault through the air. The pair make a gigantic nest called an eyrie. It is built in a tree or on a rocky cliff and made of sticks, weeds, and soil. The birds use the nest year after year and keep adding to it.

The white feathers on its head are fully visible by the time the bird is four years old.

Fish such as salmon are a common source of food for the eagle.

Bald eagle
(*Haliaeetus leucocephalus*)
Length: 3 ft 2 in (96 cm)
Wingspan: up to 8 ft (2 m 40 cm)

The maple trees of broad-leaved woodlands turn spectacular shades of red and gold before losing their leaves for the winter.

Yellow-bellied sapsucker

The yellow-bellied sapsucker drills neat rows of holes in trees, such as birches, and waits for the sap to ooze out and run down the trunk. Then it laps up the sugary sap with its brushlike tongue. Insects sometimes get trapped in the sticky liquid and the sapsucker eats these as well. In winter, the yellow-bellied sapsucker migrates south to the warmer climates of Central America and the Caribbean islands.

Yellow-bellied sapsucker
(*Sphyrapicus varius*)
Length: 8 in (21 cm)

Northern bobwhite
(*Colinus virginianus*)
Length: 11 in (28 cm)

If a covey is disturbed, the birds fly off in different directions to confuse enemies and give the birds time to escape.

Northern bobwhite

Outside the breeding season, bobwhites gather in groups of 15 to 30 birds, called coveys. Each covey defends its own special area from other coveys. At night, a covey huddles on the ground in a circle. The birds sit with their heads pointing outward to face danger and their bodies touching to keep warm.

0   250   500   750 km
0   250   500 miles

ARCTIC OCEAN

GULF OF ALASKA

PACIFIC OCEAN

Great Bear Lake

Great Slave Lake

NORTH AMERICA

ROCKY MTS

Rio Grande

YELLOW-BELLIED SAPSUCKER

NORTHERN CARDINAL

EASTERN WHIP-POOR-WILL

BALD EAGLE

RUFFED GROUSE

AMERICAN ROBIN

NORTHERN BOBWHITE

OWLS—THE NIGHT HUNTERS

Owls are one of the most characteristic birds of woodland areas. They have short, rounded wings so they can fly easily between the trees. They have large eyes and can turn their heads right around to see behind them. Most owls are night hunters, using their sharp hearing and eyesight to catch food in the dark. Many owls have round faces, which act like radar dishes, funneling the sounds to their ear openings. The openings lie under feathered flaps of skin on the sides of their faces.

Owls have powerful legs with needle-sharp, curved talons for gripping prey.

Flight feathers have a soft fringe to break up the flow of air and muffle the sound of the wings. Owls make very little noise as they fly.

The owl's outer toe can point either forward or backward for extra grip.

A woodland owl swoops silently down from a perch, swinging its feet forward to grab its prey. It swallows prey, such as mice and voles, whole, head first. It cannot digest bones, fur, or feathers, so it coughs these up as pellets.

Northern cardinal

Northern cardinals have a rich variety of songs and males and females may sing in turn as if replying to each other. Unlike other birds that live in territories just for the breeding season, cardinals sing all year to keep other birds away. The cardinal is named after the bright red robes worn by Roman Catholic cardinals.

Male

The male cardinal is more colorful than the female.

Female

Northern cardinal
(*Cardinalis cardinalis*)
Length: 9 in (23.5 cm)

Ruffed grouse

In spring, the male ruffed grouse often sits on a log and makes a drumming sound by beating his wings to and fro. The sound gets faster and faster, carrying a long way through the forest and helping attract a female. She nests among aspen trees, feeding on the tree catkins while she sits on her eggs to keep them warm. In winter, ruffed grouse grow comblike bristles on their toes that act as snowshoes.

Ruffed grouse
(*Bonasa umbellus*)
Length: 1 ft 7 in (48 cm)

Mottled feathers ensure the bird is well camouflaged among dead leaves.

Eastern whip-poor-will
(*Antrostomus vociferus*)
Length: 11 in (27 cm)

Eastern whip-poor-will

During the day, the eastern whip-poor-will sleeps on the forest floor. Its mottled colors match the dead leaves so it is hard to see. At night, it flies near the ground with its mouth open, scooping up flying insects. The bird is so named because of its call which sounds like "whip-poor-will." It may repeat the call a hundred times or more without stopping.

HUDSON BAY

St. Lawrence

ATLANTIC OCEAN

Great Lakes

APPALACHIAN MTS.

Mississippi

American robin

This robin originally nested in open woodlands but has adapted well to suburban gardens. It often builds a nest on a house porch or in a nearby tree. It eats insects and worms, but also likes fruit, especially in winter. It sometimes spends the winter in northern conifer forests, gathering in large roosts of thousands of birds.

American robins have keen eyesight for finding worms.

American robin
(*Turdus migratorius*)
Length: 11 in (28 cm)

13

Western Mountains

THE WESTERN MOUNTAIN RANGES, such as the Rockies, the Cascade Range, and the Sierra Nevada, provide a variety of habitats for birds, concentrated in a small space. The warm, wet weather on the lower mountain slopes encourages the growth of dense forests. These forests shelter and feed many birds, from woodpeckers and nutcrackers to jays and chickadees. Higher up the mountains, it is cooler and drier, and the forests give way to grassy meadows and bare, rocky ground on the frozen peaks. Here, eagles and other birds of prey soar on rising air currents, which sweep over the mountains. A few unusual birds, such as ptarmigans, survive on the higher slopes—their downy feathers keeping them warm.

Golden eagle
(*Aquila chrysaetos*)
Length: up to
3 ft (90 cm)
Wingspan: up to
7 ft 7 in
(2 m 30 cm)

Strong talons for gripping prey, such as this rabbit, and flying with it.

Powerful, hooked bill for tearing flesh from prey.

Golden eagle

To hunt for food, the golden eagle soars high up in the sky on its powerful wings. When its sharp eyes spot a small mammal, it dives quickly down to seize its prey and crush it in its hooked talons. The golden eagle will attack animals as big as deer, especially in winter when other food is scarce. It builds enormous nests on rocky crags or in tall trees.

Black-billed magpie

The black-billed magpie is an adaptable bird that eats a range of foods, especially insects and small rodents. It often perches on the backs of cattle and sheep to pick off the ticks and maggots that live on their skin. It builds a large, strong nest of twigs, mud, and plant material, lined with fine grass and hair. A dome of sticks, often thorny ones, protects the top of the nest from predators.

Tail is longer than the body.

Black-billed magpie
(*Pica hudsonia*)
Length: 2 ft (60 cm)

White-tailed ptarmigan

In winter, this ptarmigan grows white feathers, which camouflage it against the snowy landscape. It often crouches down in the snow to keep out of the fierce, cold mountain winds and to avoid predators. It tends to run away from danger instead of flying. In the summer breeding season, it grows mottled brown feathers. These are very useful to the female, as they hide her while she sits on her eggs.

White-tailed ptarmigan
(*Lagopus leucurus*)
Length: 1 ft 1 in (34 cm)

Mountain chickadee
(*Poecile gambeli*)
Length: 6 in (15 cm)

Mountain chickadee

In spring and summer, the mountain chickadee nests in the mountain forests, but it moves down to warmer valleys in the cold winter months. There it joins flocks of other small birds, such as wood warblers and vireos, that roam the valley forests searching for food. If chickadees kept to their own territories in winter, they would not find enough food to eat.

Feathers keep its feet warm. Scales on the toes act as snowshoes to stop the bird sinking into snow.

The chickadee feeds on insects and seeds in conifers, such as this Douglas fir.

Deserts

THE HOT, DRY DESERTS of the southwestern United States are home to a surprising variety of birds. To cope with the heat, birds rest in the shade of rocks or down burrows dug by desert mammals. There is not much water to drink—the Sonoran Desert receives less than 8 in (20 cm) of rain a year and the Great Basin deserts only 1½ in (4 cm) a year. Birds get most of the water they need from their food, such as seeds, other animals, and water-filled cacti. The spiny branches of cacti help protect the nests of many birds and some, such as the saguaro, are so big that birds can nest inside them, out of the heat of the sun. In the Great Basin Desert, the many sagebrush shrubs are rich in energy-giving fats for birds to eat.

A gila woodpecker perches on a giant desert cactus to feed insects to its young nesting inside.

Map labels:
GULF OF ALASKA
NORTH AMERICA
ROCKY MTS
HUDSON BAY
PACIFIC OCEAN
GREAT BASIN
DEATH VALLEY
MOJAVE DESERT
ROCKY MTS
GREAT PLAINS
Arkansas
Red River
SONORAN DESERT
Rio Grande
SIERRA MADRE OCCIDENTAL
GULF OF CALIFORNIA
GULF OF MEXICO

Map key:
- GOLDEN EAGLE
- BLACK-BILLED MAGPIE
- MOUNTAIN CHICKADEE
- ELF OWL
- CACTUS WREN
- WHITE-TAILED PTARMIGAN
- GREATER ROADRUNNER

0   200   400   600 km
0   200   400 miles

Cactus wren

This is the largest North American wren. Like other wrens, it builds several nests—some to sleep in, some to shelter in, and a few for their eggs and young. Each nest is a domed shape with a tunnellike entrance and is built on a prickly cholla cactus or a spiny yucca or mesquite tree. The wren doesn't seem to mind the sharp spines, but enemies find it hard to reach the nest.

Cactus wren
(*Campylorhynchus brunneicapillus*)
Length: 7½ in (19 cm)

Greater roadrunner

The roadrunner is really a type of cuckoo that lives on the ground. Even though it is often seen on roads, it is a shy bird that runs rapidly away from danger. It also chases anything that moves. On its long, powerful legs, it can sprint at up to 15 mph (24 kph), fluttering its stubby wings for extra speed. Its long tail acts as a brake to help the bird stop or change direction.

Elf owl
(*Micrathene whitneyi*)
Length: 5½ in (14 cm)

Elf owl

This is the smallest owl in the world—it is no bigger than an adult's hand. It feeds mainly at night, catching insects in its feet. It will also eat scorpions, taking out the sting or crushing it before starting to eat. To escape the heat of the sun, it roosts by day in holes in giant cacti dug by other birds. If captured, the elf owl pretends to be dead until it thinks the danger has passed.

Greater roadrunner
(*Geococcyx californianus*)
Length: 2 ft (58 cm)

The roadrunner has a very varied diet that includes lizards, mice, insects, and even small rattlesnakes.

The Wetlands

NORTH AMERICA'S RIVERS, lakes, marshes, and swamps, or the wetlands as they are known, are a rich environment for birds because of the variety of food and nesting places they provide. Many marshes, which were once protected so people could hunt the ducks and geese, are now nature reserves. In the southeast are swamps dominated by bald cypress trees draped with vines, Spanish moss, and orchids. These include the Florida Everglades and the bayous of the Mississippi delta. There is an amazing number of ponds and lakes in North America. Some formed where ice sheets dug hollows in the land. Others formed as a result of movements of the Earth's crust. Many rivers, lakes, and swamps are threatened by the pollution caused by farms and factories.

Whooping crane

The whooping crane is one of the world's most endangered species. It almost died out in the 1940s, but its numbers are now increasing thanks to conservation. The whooping crane nests in northwestern Canada but migrates south to the warmer weather of Texas in winter. Its name comes from its loud, trumpeting call.

Jet-black wing tips

Head and neck are stretched out in flight.

Whooping crane
(*Grus americana*)
Length: 5 ft 2 in (1 m 60 cm)

Common loon

The common loon, or great northern diver, as it is sometimes known, can plunge up to 266 ft (81 m) below the waters of lakes and rivers. Its feet are set well back on its body to push it through the water when it dives, but the bird finds it hard to walk on dry land. It sometimes produces a mournful, yodeling call or wails and laughs wildly.

In winter, the loon's plumage is much paler and duller than it is in summer.

Common loon
(*Gavia immer*)
Length: 3 ft (91 cm)

Winter

Summer

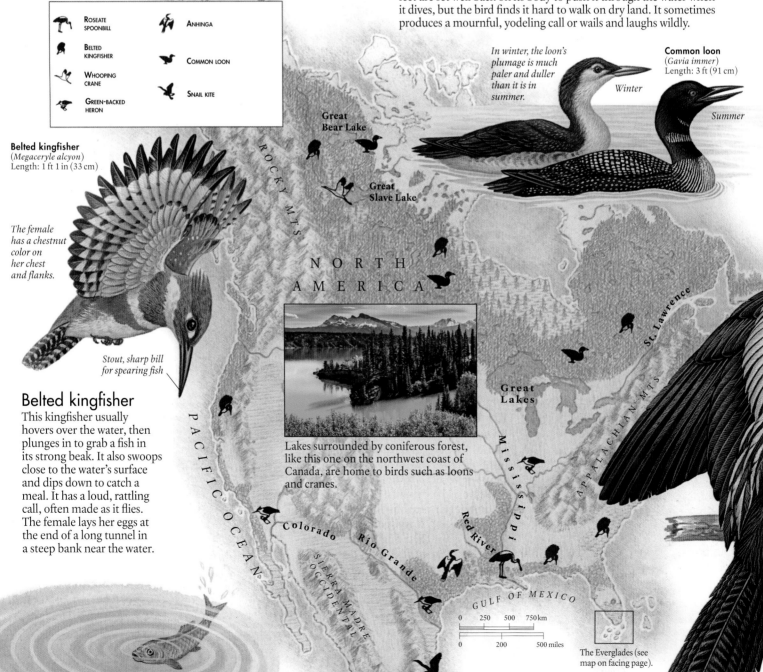

ROSEATE SPOONBILL		ANHINGA	
BELTED KINGFISHER		COMMON LOON	
WHOOPING CRANE		SNAIL KITE	
GREEN-BACKED HERON			

Belted kingfisher
(*Megaceryle alcyon*)
Length: 1 ft 1 in (33 cm)

The female has a chestnut color on her chest and flanks.

Stout, sharp bill for spearing fish

Belted kingfisher

This kingfisher usually hovers over the water, then plunges in to grab a fish in its strong beak. It also swoops close to the water's surface and dips down to catch a meal. It has a loud, rattling call, often made as it flies. The female lays her eggs at the end of a long tunnel in a steep bank near the water.

Great Bear Lake

Great Slave Lake

ROCKY MTS

NORTH AMERICA

St. Lawrence

Great Lakes

APPALACHIAN MTS

PACIFIC OCEAN

Lakes surrounded by coniferous forest, like this one on the northwest coast of Canada, are home to birds such as loons and cranes.

Colorado

Rio Grande

SIERRA MADRE OCCIDENTAL

Red River

Mississippi

GULF OF MEXICO

0	250	500	750km

0	200	500 miles

The Everglades (see map on facing page).

The Everglades

The tropical swamps of the Everglades National Park in southern Florida are home to a unique variety of birds. Many migrating birds stop and rest here, too. The whole area is only just above sea level and consists of a huge swamp covered with sedges, grasses, and rushes. Deeper channels of open water run through it. These contain islands of trees called hummocks. Along the coast, belts of mangrove trees trap mud and silt with their roots and build up new land. The birds feed on the variety of insects and fish that live in this warm, humid environment.

In the swampy waters of the Everglades, islands of trees occur on slightly higher ground. The dense plant growth gives protection from storms and floods.

EVERGLADES

GULF
OF
MEXICO

FLORIDA
BAY

FLORIDA KEYS

ATLANTIC
OCEAN

0 10 20 30 km
0   10   20 miles

Snail kite

This unusual kite feeds mainly on water snails. It flaps slowly over the swamps on its large, wide wings. When it spots a snail, it swoops down, grabs the snail in one foot, and carries it to a perch. Then it uses its thin, hooked bill to pull out the body of the snail without breaking the shell. Snail kites in the Everglades were once near extinction but are now protected.

Snail kite
(*Rostrhamus sociabilis*)
Length: 1 ft 7 in (48 cm)

Long, hooked upper bill

Male has red legs; female and young have orange legs.

Roseate spoonbill

Spoonbills have elaborate courtship displays, including clapping bills and giving each other twigs. To catch food, the spoonbill sweeps its sensitive bill from side to side through the water. When it feels food, such as fish, it snaps its bill quickly shut. Spoonbills were once hunted for their feathers, which were used to decorate hats. They are now protected and their numbers have grown.

Roseate spoonbill
(*Platalea ajaja*)
Length: 2 ft 10 in (86.5 cm)

Broad tip of the long bill is like a spoon.

Ear opening on the side of the head

Green-backed heron

The shy green-backed heron feeds mainly at night and hides among waterside plants by day. But it has adapted well to living in urban areas near people. This wading bird grabs fish and small animals in its long, strong bill and will sometimes dive underwater to chase its prey.

Crest is raised when the bird is excited.

Anhinga

The anhinga often swims on the surface with just its head and neck showing, so it looks like a snake. It dives deep under the water to catch fish, spearing them with its daggerlike bill. The jagged edges of its bill help the anhinga keep a firm hold on its prey, until it can flip it up into the air and swallow it whole.

The female has a tawny colored neck and breast.

Large, broad wings are spread out to dry in the sun.

Anhinga
(*Anhinga anhinga*)
Length: 3 ft (91 cm)

The green-backed heron often crouches, silent and still, at the edge of water to spot its prey.

Green-backed heron
(*Butorides striata*)
Length: 1 ft 7 in (48 cm)

Central America and the Caribbean

THE RICH BIRD LIFE of Central America is partly due to the landscapes in the region, which vary from dry grassland on the west coast to alpine meadows in the middle and lush rainforest and swamps on the eastern coasts. Central America forms a narrow bridge linking North and South America, so birds from both continents mix there. Many North American birds migrate to the warmer climate of Central America for the winter.

The Caribbean islands are the tips of mountains buried in very deep water. The birds here are either strong fliers that were able to reach the islands or they were blown there accidentally by strong winds. Several unique species have developed on the islands: the tody family, for example, is found nowhere else in the world.

The male has shiny feathers and shimmers from head to tail.

The female is dull colored and does not have a long tail.

Resplendent quetzal

The ancient peoples of Central America, the Maya and the Aztecs, worshipped the quetzal as a sacred bird. Today it is the national bird of Guatemala. Quetzals usually live on their own, searching for fruit or insects in forest trees. The male has extraordinary tail feathers to help him attract a female.

Resplendent quetzal
(*Pharomachrus mocinno*)
Length: 1 ft 4 in (40 cm)

Black skimmer	Three-wattled bellbird
Oilbird	Puerto Rican tody
Crested oropendola	Resplendent quetzal
Sunbittern	

A male grows new tail feathers each breeding season. They can be up to 2 ft (60 cm) long.

NORTH AMERICA

Arkansas

Red River

Mississippi

ROCKY MTS

SIERRA MADRE OCCIDENTAL

Large, sensitive eyes for finding its way about at night.

GULF OF MEXICO

BAHAMAS

ATLANTIC OCEAN

CUBA

HISPANIOLA

PUERTO RICO

GREATER ANTILLES

JAMAICA

LESSER ANTILLES

CARIBBEAN SEA

Small, weak legs and feet

Oilbird
(*Steatornis caripensis*)
Length: 1 ft 7 in (49 cm)

Orinoco

CENTRAL AMERICA

GULF OF PANAMA

PACIFIC OCEAN

ANDES

Rio Negro

Oilbird

Young oilbirds do not fly until they are about four months old so they grow incredibly fat. People used to make oil from their fatty flesh, which is how the bird got its name. The oilbird lives in caves and finds its way in the darkness by making clicking sounds. The time it takes for the sound to bounce back lets the bird work out how far away walls or objects are. At night, it flies out of the cave to feed on oily fruits. Its good sense of smell and excellent eyesight help it find food.

0	200	400	600 km

0	200	400 miles

Each woven nest is over 3 ft 3 in (1 m) long and hangs from a tree branch.

Mouth opens very wide to allow the bird to swallow large fruits.

Three-wattled bellbird

Male bellbirds make one of the loudest calls of any bird. They advertise for a female by producing an explosive "bock" noise. This call can be heard 0.6 miles (1 km) away. The female builds the nest and looks after the young. She is a dull color to camouflage her while she sits on the nest.

Wattles hang from top of bill and edge of mouth.

Three-wattled bellbird
(*Procnias tricarunculatus*)
Length: 1 ft (30 cm)

Crested oropendola

Crested oropendolas live in groups and nest together, too. They can build up to 100 nests in just one tree. This probably helps protect the eggs and young from predators, as the birds can warn each other of danger. The male has a spectacular courtship display to attract a female. He makes a series of loud gurgling sounds while flapping his wings and leaning forward so far that he almost falls off his perch.

Constantly jerks head while perched.

Long, straight bill for snapping up insects.

Crested oropendola
(*Psarocolius decumanus*)
Length: 1 ft 7 in (48 cm)

Puerto Rican tody

This tody lives in woods and forests and feeds by pouncing on insects from a perch. When it flies, it makes a whirring noise with its wings. During the breeding season, the tody uses its bill to dig tiny nesting burrows in a bank, like its relative the kingfisher. There are four other species of Caribbean tody.

Puerto Rican tody
(*Todus mexicanus*)
Length: 5 in (12 cm)

Sunbittern

During its courtship display, the sunbittern spreads its wings to show off the patches of orange and yellow on its feathers. These look like the colors of a sky at sunset, which is how the bird got its name. At other times, the mottled colors on the feathers camouflage the bird as it searches for food along stream banks in woodland areas. It catches fish, insects, and frogs with its long, sharp bill.

Wings are spread out during courtship displays.

Sunbittern
(*Eurypyga helias*)
Length: 1 ft 7 in (48 cm)

Black skimmer
(*Rynchops niger*)
Length: 1 ft 6 in
(46 cm)

Dense jungle vegetation is typical of Central America's tropical rainforests.

Amazon

Tapajós

Black skimmer

The black skimmer has a strange bill—the bottom part is about one-third longer than the top part. To find food, the skimmer flies over shallow water with its bill open. When its bill hits a small fish or crustacean, the skimmer snaps the top bill down to trap its prey.

The Amazon Rainforest

THE AMAZON RAINFOREST stretches from the Andes Mountains in the west to the Atlantic Ocean in the east. One-fifth of all the kinds of birds in the world live there. This is mainly due to differences in rainfall, soils, and height of the land across the region, which provide a variety of habitats. Birds live at different layers in the trees, rather like people live in a block of flats. Each layer receives different amounts of sunlight and provides different kinds of food. Birds such as toucans live in the tree-tops, called the canopy. In the middle layers live birds such as macaws and jacamars, while down on the forest floor larger birds stalk among the fallen leaves.

Red-billed toucan

With its long bill, the red-billed toucan can reach out to pluck berries or seeds from trees high in the canopy. The jagged edges of its bill work like a saw to cut fruits. It also eats insects, spiders, and small birds. Its bill is hollow and extremely light. The brightly coloured bill may help it recognize others of its kind.

Red-billed toucan
(*Ramphastos tucanus*)
Length: 2 ft (58 cm)

Scarlet macaw

At sunrise the scarlet macaw flies through the forest in search of food. It squawks noisily while flying but feeds in silence. Two of its toes point forward and two point backward, so it can use its feet to grip well and hold food up to its mouth.

The macaw's powerful bill can crush the hardest seeds and nuts. It is also used for preening and to grip branches.

Scarlet macaw
(*Ara macao*)
Length: 2 ft 11 in (89 cm)

Short legs help the macaw keep its balance.

Guianan cock-of-the-rock

The male Guianan cock-of-the-rock performs amazing displays on the forest floor to attract a female. Up to 25 males display together and each has his own area. They show off by leaping into the air, bobbing their heads, snapping their bills, and flicking and fanning their feathers.

Guianan cock-of-the-rock
(*Rupicola rupicola*)
Length: 1 ft 1 in
(32 cm)

Female cock-of-the-rocks are drab colored for camouflage and look very different from males.

During his display the male spreads his crest forward so it almost hides his bill.

The male displays on a bare patch of forest floor called a "lek."

ATLANTIC
OCEAN

Orinoco

AMAZON
RAINFOREST

Rio Negro

Amazon

Amazon

SOUTH

AMERICA

PACIFIC
OCEAN

A
N
D
E
S

*Lake
Titicaca*

	HARPY EAGLE		WHITE-PLUMED ANTBIRD
	RUFOUS-BREASTED HERMIT		SCARLET MACAW
	HOATZIN		GUIANAN COCK-OF-THE-ROCK
	RED-BILLED TOUCAN		

0	200	400	800 km

0	250		500 miles

Rainforest birds are often brightly colored but they are hard to see against a background of leaves and patches of sunlight.

Two toes point forward and two point backward to give a strong grip.

Toucans live in groups and often play games. They wrestle with their bills or toss fruit to each other.

Powerful, hooked bill for tearing flesh from food.

Harpy eagle
(*Harpia harpyja*)
Length: 3 ft 4 in (1 m)

Harpy eagle

The huge and fearsome harpy eagle swoops through the treetops seeking its prey. It can fly at speeds of up to 50 mph (80 kph). Its gray, mottled coloring helps camouflage it among the leaves so the animals it hunts do not see it coming. Harpy eagles build nests made of sticks high up in the trees.

Massive sharp talons enable the eagle to grab and crush prey.

The harpy eagle pursues capuchin monkeys and other small animals, such as opossums and coatis, through the rainforest.

White-plumed antbird

Despite its name, the white-plumed antbird does not eat ants. It follows army ants and feeds on the spiders and insects that are trying to escape them. Usually the antbird darts down to the ground or hangs from a branch to snatch up a meal. But sometimes it will hop among the ants, holding its tail up out of the way. Its long legs help protect its body from the ants' stings.

Rufous-breasted hermit

The hermit is a kind of hummingbird. The hermit's thin, curved bill probes flowers for nectar, which flows into the grooves of its long tongue as it flicks in and out. Nectar is easy to digest so it provides instant energy to power the hummingbird's whirring wings, and also helps the bird generate body warmth.

Rufous-breasted hermit
(*Glaucis hirsutus*)
Length: 5 in (12 cm)

White-plumed antbird
(*Pithys albifrons*)
Length: 5 in (12.5 cm)

Hoatzin

The hoatzin has weak wings and it flaps clumsily through flooded parts of the rainforest along quiet riverbanks. It uses its wings and tail to help it clamber through the trees as its feet are not very strong. Hoatzins move about and nest in groups, building untidy twig nests by the water. Young hoatzins leave the nest soon after hatching and may leap into the water to escape danger. Hoatzins feed mostly on leaves and have multichambered stomachs, like cows, to digest them.

Hoatzin
(*Opisthocomus hoazin*)
Length: 2 ft 3 in (70 cm)

The antbird often perches on a small tree and waits for ants to appear.

Columns of army ants swarming over the forest floor.

A baby hoatzin has two tiny claws on the bend of each wing to help it grip and climb.

The Andes

THE ANDES ARE THE WORLD'S longest mountain chain, running down the entire western coast of South America. The steep slopes act as a barrier to birds, so species on the east side of the mountains differ from those on the west. Plant life in the Andes also varies dramatically over short distances, creating a variety of habitats. These range from rainforests on the lower slopes, through drier forests and grass plains higher up, to frozen wilderness near the peaks. On the upper slopes, it is so cold that some hummingbirds go into torpor at night—a kind of deep sleep where they slow down all their body processes and lower their body temperature, so they use less energy.

Andean condor

This huge vulture is the world's heaviest bird of prey, weighing up to 31 lb (14 kg). The Andean condor soars for long distances on outstretched wings, sometimes rising to heights of 23,000 ft (7,000 m) over the mountains. It has very keen eyesight and can spot dead animals to feed on from high up in the sky. It will also kill sick or wounded animals. Some Andean condors raid seabird colonies on the coast and take the eggs and chicks.

Andean condor
(*Vultur gryphus*)
Length: 4 ft 3 in (1 m 30 cm)
Wingspan: up to 10 ft 4 in (3 m 20 cm)

The condor probably has the greatest wingspan of any land bird.

Bare head enables the bird to reach into a carcass without getting its feathers dirty.

Sword-billed hummingbird

This bird's extraordinary bill enables it to reach nectar and insects deep inside trumpet-shaped flowers. As the hummingbird hovers below the flowers to feed, pollen is caught on its feathers and the bird then carries this to other flowers, pollinating the plants (helping them produce seeds). Over half the flowers in the high Andes are pollinated by hummingbirds instead of insects.

Sword-billed hummingbird
(*Ensifera ensifera*)
Length: 3 in (7.5 cm)
Length of bill: 4 in (10.5 cm)

Long bill for reaching pollen inside fuchsias and other trumpet-shaped flowers.

Torrent duck

The fast-flowing rivers and streams of the Andes are home to the torrent duck. Its sharp claws and powerful legs help it cling to slippery rocks, while its stiff tail is useful for balancing and steering in the water. It dives underwater to catch food, such as insects, but it also picks up food as it floats past on the surface. Ducklings are able to swim with their parents as soon as they hatch.

Torrent duck
(*Merganetta armata*)
Length: 1 ft 6 in (46 cm)

Streamlined body shape for swimming fast under the water.

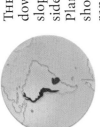

Areas of dense rainforest shrouded in mist cover the lower slopes of the Andes.

SOUTH AMERICA

CARIBBEAN SEA

São Francisco

Madeira

Rio Negro

Amazon

Japurá

Marañón

Ucayali

ANDES

750 km 500 miles
250 500
250
0 0

SOUTHERN CARACARA BURROWING OWL GREATER RHEA

TORRENT DUCK ANDEAN CONDOR SWORD-BILLED HUMMINGBIRD RUFOUS HORNERO

Greater rhea

The rhea is very similar to the African ostrich, except that it has three toes on each foot instead of two. It cannot fly, but it can sprint faster than a horse, reaching speeds of 31 mph (50 kph). In the breeding season, males fight for territory and for females. Several females lay their eggs in one male's nest and he looks after the eggs and chicks.

Rheas have three strong toes with claws on each foot for defense and for running fast.

Long legs for running swiftly if necessary.

Southern caracara
(*Caracara plancus*)
Length: 2 ft 1 in (64 cm)

Burrowing owl

Unlike most owls, burrowing owls are often active during the day. They usually live in other animals' abandoned mud burrows and spend a lot of time perched at the entrance. If disturbed, they bob up and down and make a chattering noise. Burrowing owls can run quickly over the grasslands on their long legs to catch their food, which is usually insects and small reptiles.

This owl nests in burrows made by viscachas and other animals, but it can also dig its own.

Greater rhea
(*Rhea americana*)
Length: 4 ft 6 in (1 m 40 cm)
Height: 5 ft (1 m 50 cm)

Southern caracara

These chicken-sized birds of prey are related to falcons. Caracaras build their own nests, unlike true falcons that use abandoned nests. They eat a varied diet from small mammals, birds, fish, and frogs to insects and dead meat—they often join vultures to feed on a carcass. Caracaras are slow and lazy birds, but they have long legs and can move quickly if in danger.

Burrowing owl
(*Athene cunicularia*)
Length: 10 in (26 cm)

The Pampas

The grassy plains of the pampas lie in the southeastern corner of South America. The climate is generally dry with hot summers and cool winters. Lightning can cause fires in the dry grass, and farmers also set fire to the grass to encourage new shoots to grow, so some birds nest under the ground where they are safer from fires and people. Large cattle ranches on the pampas have damaged the natural environment. Only birds that can adapt to human disturbance, such as ovenbirds, have survived. Others have died out or decreased in number. Huge flocks of rheas are no longer common.

The vast, treeless plains of the pampas provide little shelter for birds, so they nest by rocks or under the ground.

Rufous hornero

The mud nest of the rufous hornero looks like an old-fashioned baker's oven, so these birds are sometimes called ovenbirds. (The word *hornero* means "baker" in Spanish.) It takes the bird months to build one nest, and yet it starts a new one each year. The rufous hornero has long legs and strides across open ground lifting its feet high in the air. It uses its strong, sharp bill to dig up worms and insect larvae.

Rufous hornero
(*Furnarius rufus*)
Length: 9 in (23 cm)

The nest is made of thousands of lumps of mud, reinforced with straw and baked hard in the hot sun.

Lake Titicaca

PACIFIC OCEAN

Paraná

Uruguay

Paraná

PAMPAS

ANDES

The Galápagos Islands

THE LONELY GALÁPAGOS ISLANDS, which lie in the Pacific Ocean, west of South America, are like nowhere else on Earth. An extraordinary variety of birds live among the dry cactus scrub and jagged volcanic rocks, and many of them are found only on these islands. There are two main reasons why the bird life of the Galápagos Islands is so unique. Firstly, the islands are so far from the mainland of South America that only a few birds have managed to reach them. These were able to develop into a variety of species because there was little competition for food and nesting places. Secondly, warm waters from the Pacific and cool waters from the Antarctic both flow past the islands. This means that birds usually found in cold places, such as penguins and albatrosses, live side-by-side with tropical species, such as flamingos and frigate birds.

ISLA
MARCHENA

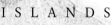

GALÁPAGOS

ISLANDS

ISLA SAN
SALVADOR

ISLA
FERNANDINA

The frigate bird has the greatest wingspan of any bird, in relation to the size of its body.

ISLA
ISABELA

Tiny wings only 10 in (25 cm) long

PACIFIC
OCEAN

Flightless cormorant
(*Nannopterum harrisi*)
Length: 3 ft 3 in (1 m)

Flightless cormorant

The flightless cormorant uses its small, ragged wings to balance on land and to shade its chick from the hot sun, but its wings are too weak for flying or swimming. It probably lost its ability to fly because it had no enemies to fly away from and could get all its food close to the shore. Now it is the only cormorant alive that cannot fly. This made it easy for people to hunt it, so it became rare. Today it is a protected species.

They nest on rocks close to the sea.

DARWIN'S FINCHES

The 18 different species of Galápagos finch look similar because they probably originated from one species. But each species has a different shaped bill to eat a different food. The British naturalist Charles Darwin's studies of these birds helped him develop his theory of evolution. This explains how plants and animals may have changed over many generations to suit their particular habitat.

**Charles
Darwin**
1809–1882

Gray warbler-finch
(*Certhidea fusca*)
This finch has a fine, pointed bill for catching small insects.

Small tree finch
(*Geospiza parvula*)
The tree finch has a thicker bill to cope with fruit, buds, small seeds, and insects.

Large ground finch
(*Geospiza magnirostris*)
This large ground finch has a heavy, strong bill for crushing seeds.

Woodpecker finch
(*Geospiza pallida*)
This is one of the few birds to make and use a tool. It uses a twig as a tool to find insect grubs under bark and tease them out.

Galápagos penguin

This rare penguin is able to live so near the equator because of the cool waters of the Humboldt Current, which flow past the Galápagos Islands. It feeds on fish and nests in small groups, laying its eggs in nests of stones, in caves, or in holes. It has flipper-like wings, webbed feet, and a streamlined body shape, which make it a very strong swimmer, but it is clumsy on land. It hops shakily from one rock to another, holding out its little flippers for balance. When it reaches the water, it jumps in feet first.

Strong flippers help the penguin "fly" underwater.

Galápagos penguin
(*Spheniscus mendiculus*)
Length: 1 ft 8 in (53 cm)

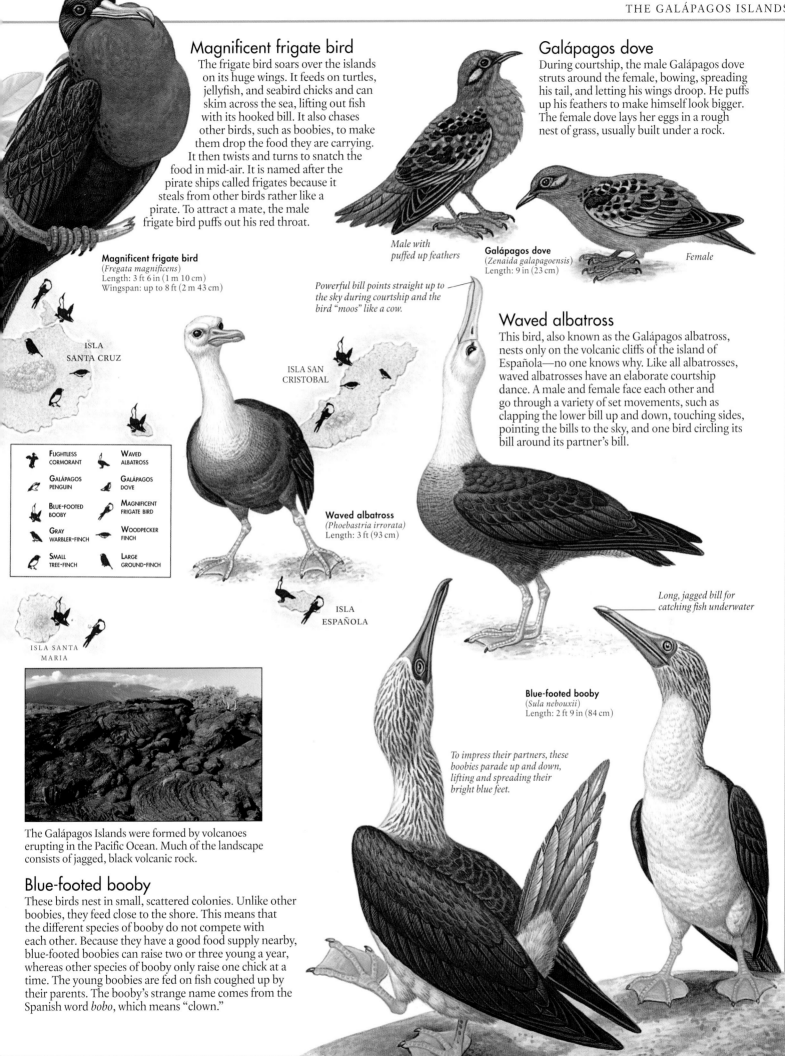

Magnificent frigate bird

The frigate bird soars over the islands on its huge wings. It feeds on turtles, jellyfish, and seabird chicks and can skim across the sea, lifting out fish with its hooked bill. It also chases other birds, such as boobies, to make them drop the food they are carrying. It then twists and turns to snatch the food in mid-air. It is named after the pirate ships called frigates because it steals from other birds rather like a pirate. To attract a mate, the male frigate bird puffs out his red throat.

Magnificent frigate bird
(*Fregata magnificens*)
Length: 3 ft 6 in (1 m 10 cm)
Wingspan: up to 8 ft (2 m 43 cm)

Galápagos dove

During courtship, the male Galápagos dove struts around the female, bowing, spreading his tail, and letting his wings droop. He puffs up his feathers to make himself look bigger. The female dove lays her eggs in a rough nest of grass, usually built under a rock.

Male with puffed up feathers

Galápagos dove
(*Zenaida galapagoensis*)
Length: 9 in (23 cm)

Female

Powerful bill points straight up to the sky during courtship and the bird "moos" like a cow.

Waved albatross

This bird, also known as the Galápagos albatross, nests only on the volcanic cliffs of the island of Española—no one knows why. Like all albatrosses, waved albatrosses have an elaborate courtship dance. A male and female face each other and go through a variety of set movements, such as clapping the lower bill up and down, touching sides, pointing the bills to the sky, and one bird circling its bill around its partner's bill.

Waved albatross
(*Phoebastria irrorata*)
Length: 3 ft (93 cm)

ISLA SANTA CRUZ

ISLA SAN CRISTOBAL

ISLA ESPAÑOLA

ISLA SANTA MARIA

FLIGHTLESS CORMORANT
WAVED ALBATROSS
GALÁPAGOS PENGUIN
GALÁPAGOS DOVE
BLUE-FOOTED BOOBY
MAGNIFICENT FRIGATE BIRD
GRAY WARBLER-FINCH
WOODPECKER FINCH
SMALL TREE-FINCH
LARGE GROUND-FINCH

Long, jagged bill for catching fish underwater

Blue-footed booby
(*Sula nebouxii*)
Length: 2 ft 9 in (84 cm)

To impress their partners, these boobies parade up and down, lifting and spreading their bright blue feet.

The Galápagos Islands were formed by volcanoes erupting in the Pacific Ocean. Much of the landscape consists of jagged, black volcanic rock.

Blue-footed booby

These birds nest in small, scattered colonies. Unlike other boobies, they feed close to the shore. This means that the different species of booby do not compete with each other. Because they have a good food supply nearby, blue-footed boobies can raise two or three young a year, whereas other species of booby only raise one chick at a time. The young boobies are fed on fish coughed up by their parents. The booby's strange name comes from the Spanish word *bobo*, which means "clown."

EUROPE

THE SMALL CONTINENT of Europe has been covered by ice at least four times in the past million years. The climate in northern Europe is still very cold and many birds from this region migrate south for the winter.

Europe does not have a huge variety of bird species, partly due to the cold weather in the north, but also because of the large numbers of people that live there—many more than in North America. People have cleared away the forests, polluted the land and water, and hunted the birds. Birds that cannot live in cities, parks, or yards have been driven to remote areas such as mountains, moorlands, and marshes. Many coastal habitats in Europe are, however, very rich in bird life. Estuaries provide vital feeding and resting areas for waterbirds and waders migrating south from the Arctic. Sea cliffs are home to nesting colonies of seabirds such as gannets, guillemots, puffins, and razorbills.

Europe under ice

At various times in Earth's history, there have been cold spells called ice ages, each lasting for thousands of years. During an ice age, ice sheets and glaciers spread across Earth's surface. Over the past 900,000 years, there have been about 10 major ice ages. At the height of the last ice age, about 18,000 years ago, huge ice sheets spread out from the North Pole, covering much of Europe. Some birds died out, while others moved south to warmer places. About 11,000 years ago, the climate became warmer again, the ice receded, and some of the birds returned north.

This map shows the extent of the ice sheet 11,000 years ago—at the end of Europe's last ice age.

Climate and landscape

The climate of Europe ranges from the cold, rainy, and snowy northern lands, such as Scandinavia, to the hot, dry Mediterranean lands of the south, such as Italy and Greece. In the middle are warm, wet areas with a mild climate. A warm ocean current called the Gulf Stream flows from the Caribbean past the western shores of Europe, making the winter climate on the west coast less severe. Europe's landscape includes long mountain chains, such as the Alps and the Pyrenees, which can interrupt the movement of birds from north to south.

AMAZING BIRDS OF EUROPE

Goldcrest
(*Regulus regulus*)

Smallest bird
The tiny goldcrest and its cousin the firecrest are the smallest European birds.

Fastest bird
The peregrine falcon is the fastest bird in the world. It reaches speeds of up to 112 mph (180 kph) when swooping down to chase its prey.

Long legs
Second only to flamingos, the black-winged stilt has long legs in relation to the length of its body. It can feed in very deep water.

Varied eggs
Guillemots have one of the widest varieties of colors and patterns on their eggs. This allows parents to recognize their own eggs on the crowded cliff ledges where they nest.

Largest clutch
The female gray partridge lays the most eggs at one time of any bird—as many as 15–19 eggs in one clutch. She lays so many because a large proportion of the chicks do not survive.

Marvellous mimic
The marsh warbler can imitate the calls of more than 200 other bird species.

Greatest stamina
The common swift spends more time in the air than any other land bird. It can sleep, eat, and drink while in flight, at heights of up to 6,500 ft (2,000 m).

Swift
(*Apus apus*)

Many people live and farm in the sunny Mediterranean region, growing trees such as these olives. This means there are fewer places for birds to live.

GREENLAND

ICELAND

NORTH SEA

BRITISH ISLES

Rhine

Danube

ATLANTIC OCEAN

Loire

ALPS

CORSICA

PYRENEES

SARDINIA

Douro

Guadalquivir

MEDITERRANEAN SEA

ATLAS MTS

NORTH AFRICA

FACTS ABOUT EUROPE

Longest coastline
Europe has a longer coastline in proportion to its size than any other continent. Norway's coastline is indented with steep valleys called fjords (above) that were cut into the cliffs by thick glaciers during the last ice age.

Number of birds
More than 800 species of bird have been spotted in Europe. Of these, about 430 birds are regularly seen there.

Longest glacier
The longest glacier in the Alps is called the Aletsch and is more than 15 miles (24 km) long.

High population
Europe only occupies about 7 percent of the world's land area, and has about 10 percent of the world's 7.8 billion people.

Main mountains
Mont Blanc is 15,770 ft (4,807 m) tall and is western Europe's highest mountain. It forms part of the Alps mountain range, which stretches for 680 miles (1,100 km).

Volcanic eruptions
The only active volcano on mainland Europe is Vesuvius, in Italy. It began erupting 10,000 years ago and buried the towns of Pompeii and Stabiae in 79 CE.

Longest rivers
The longest rivers in Europe are: the Volga— 2,194 miles (3,531 km); the Danube— 1,776 miles (2,858 km); and the Dnieper—1,420 miles (2,285 km) long.

Largest sea
Europe's Mediterranean Sea is the largest sea in the world.

Typical birds

Here are a few examples of typical birds from the most important habitats of Europe. These range from dark conifer forests in the north, to more open broad-leaved woodlands further south, and dry scrubland around the shores of the Mediterranean. Rivers, lakes, marshes, and coasts are also major European bird habitats.

Moorland
Birds such as this merlin nest on European moors in summer. In winter, they move to marshlands and shores where there is more food available.

Mountains
Mountains provide refuges from towns and farms for birds such as this chough, as well as golden eagles and vultures.

Coasts
Seabirds such as this puffin, along with guillemots, gulls, gannets, and terns, nest in densely packed colonies on cliffs, beaches, and islands around the coasts of Europe in spring and summer.

Mediterranean scrub
The rich variety of insects in the Mediterranean scrublands in summer attracts insect-eating birds, such as this hoopoe, along with rollers, shrikes, and honey buzzards.

Towns and cities
Birds such as this pigeon, as well as starlings, sparrows, and kestrels, have made themselves at home in urban habitats. Pigeons nest on the window ledges of tall buildings as if they were cliffs by the coast.

Estuaries and shores
In winter, waders such as this redshank, along with godwits, dunlin, and curlews, gather in flocks on estuaries and shores to feed on creatures in the mud and sand.

Forests and woodlands
Warblers such as the wood warbler, along with thrushes, jays, woodpeckers, owls, and tits, are common in the remaining areas of European forests and woodlands.

E U R O P E

CARPATHIAN MTS

Dnieper

Don

URAL MTS

Volga

A S I A

Danube

BLACK SEA

CAUCASUS MTS

CASPIAN SEA

ARAL SEA

Tigris

CYPRUS

Euphrates

MEDITERRANEAN SEA

Forests and Woodlands

FROM THE EVERGREEN forests of the north to the broad-leaved woodlands further south, European forests provide a rich habitat for birds. Tree trunks and branches are safe nesting places and tree leaves, nuts, and berries are good to eat. Insects and small creatures living on the trees and woodland floor are also food for birds. The northern forests are generally darker and colder than those further south, which have a greater variety of food and nesting places. Unfortunately, many of Europe's forests are now threatened by pollution and deforestation.

European forest and woodland birds have to arrange their lives around the seasons. In spring and summer, they nest and rear their young; in fall, they eat as much as possible to build up stores of fat in their bodies; and in winter, they may fly south to warmer places or roam widely through the forest in search of food.

Eurasian jay

The harsh, screeching call of the Eurasian jay can often be heard in broad-leaved woodlands, especially in the spring, when birds chase each other noisily through the trees as part of their courtship display. Jays feed on acorns, which they often carry for long distances, and then bury to eat during the cold winter months. Acorns that are not eaten grow into new oak trees, helping the woodlands spread. Jays also eat other nuts, berries, worms, spiders, and the eggs and young of other birds.

Crest is often raised, making the bird's head look like a square shape.

Eurasian jay
(*Garrulus glandarius*)
Length: 1 ft 3 in (37 cm)

Eurasian sparrowhawk

The agile sparrowhawk makes swift, surprise attacks on blue tits and other small birds. They stand very little chance of escaping its needle-sharp talons. Before eating its prey, the sparrowhawk plucks off the bird's feathers. The female tears up food that the male has caught to feed to the young.

The female is larger than the male and has gray bars underneath.

Blue tits

Short, rounded wings allow the bird to twist and turn through trees.

Eurasian sparrowhawk
(*Accipiter nisus*)
Length: up to 1 ft 4 in (40 cm)

| 0 | 100 | 200 | 300 km |
| 0 | | 100 | 200 miles |

Crossbills nest and feed high in the treetops of coniferous forests. They pull seeds from pine cones and rarely venture down to the forest floor.

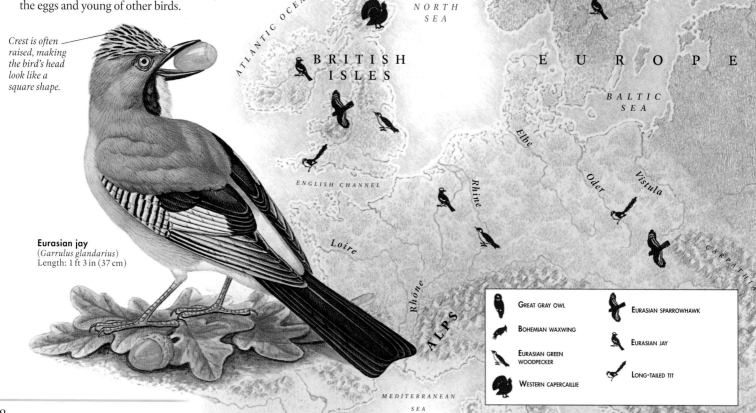

ATLANTIC OCEAN

NORTH SEA

BRITISH ISLES

EUROPE

BALTIC SEA

ENGLISH CHANNEL

Elbe

Oder

Vistula

Rhine

Loire

Rhône

ALPS

CARPATHIAN MTS

MEDITERRANEAN SEA

	GREAT GRAY OWL		EURASIAN SPARROWHAWK
	BOHEMIAN WAXWING		EURASIAN JAY
	EURASIAN GREEN WOODPECKER		LONG-TAILED TIT
	WESTERN CAPERCAILLIE		

Long-tailed tit

The tiny long-tailed tit flits about in flocks, feeding on insects, spiders, and seeds. In spring, it builds an elaborate nest of moss, cobwebs, and hair, lined with thousands of feathers to keep its young warm. The nest is so small that adult birds have to fold their tails over their heads to fit inside.

The tit's tail is longer than the body.

Long-tailed tit
(*Aegithalos caudatus*)
Length: 6 in (16 cm)

Large circles of feathers on the face collect sounds, like a radar dish.

Great gray owl

This huge owl uses its sharp hearing to detect voles on the forest floor. Even in winter, it can hear them run through tunnels beneath deep snow. The great gray owl defends its nest fiercely and will even strike people, if they get too close. The owlets leave the nest at 3–4 weeks old but take a week or so longer to learn how to fly.

Great gray owl
(*Strix nebulosa*)
Length: up to 2 ft 2 in (67 cm)
Wingspan: over 5 ft (1 m 50 cm)

During his courtship display, the male western capercaillie fans out his tail, points his bill in the air, and puffs out his throat feathers.

Western capercaillie
(*Tetrao urogallus*)
Length: male 3 ft 9 in (1 m 15 cm);
female 2 ft 1 in (64 cm)

Lake Onega

Volga

Comblike fringes on its toes may help the bird walk on snow without sinking in.

Tiny, red, waxlike blobs on the wings.

Western capercaillie

This bird lives in conifer forests, feeding on pine seeds and needles in winter and leaves, stems, and berries in summer. It nests on the forest floor. During his courtship display, the male challenges rival males with an extraordinary song, which ends with a popping and gurgling sound—like a cork being pulled out of a bottle and the drink being poured.

Male has black and red "mustache"; female's mustache is all black.

Eurasian green woodpecker

This bird is sometimes called the "yaffle," after its loud, laughing call. It has a large, daggerlike bill for probing ant hills or boring into tree trunks, and a very long tongue for licking up the insects hidden inside. It also eats fruit and seeds. During courtship, pairs of green woodpeckers spiral around trees.

Eurasian green woodpecker
(*Picus viridis*)
Length: 1 ft 1 in (33 cm)

These woodpeckers spend a lot of time on the ground searching for ants.

Bohemian waxwing
(*Bombycilla garrulus*)
Length: 9 in (23 cm)

Bohemian waxwing

The red tips on some of this bird's wing feathers look like sealing wax, which explains why it is called a waxwing. The waxwing lives in groups and chatters loudly in the breeding season. During courtship, male and female birds pass food from bill to bill. Its food is mainly the fruit and berries of woodland trees and shrubs.

Hawthorn berries are a favorite food.

The Mediterranean

IN SOUTHERN EUROPE and around the shores of the Mediterranean Sea, the climate is warmer and drier than it is farther north. People have cleared most of the forests that originally grew here, leaving small evergreen trees, thorny shrubs, heathers, and scented herbs in their place. During the long, hot summers, the air is alive with buzzing insects, which provide a rich food supply for warblers, bee-eaters, rollers, and other insect-eating birds. Large numbers of birds, such as storks, buzzards, and eagles, pass through the Mediterranean region as they migrate between Europe and Africa. The area also has some important marshland nature reserves, in particular, the Camargue in France and the Coto de Doñana in southern Spain.

The roller swoops down from a perch to catch insects.

European roller
(*Coracias garrulus*)
Length: 1 ft 1 in (32 cm)

European roller

Rollers are named after the male's rolling display flight—he flies up high then dives down, rocking from side to side and somersaulting through the air. The European roller eats mainly insects, but also hunts for lizards, snails, frogs, and other birds. In the fall, it migrates south to Africa.

Eurasian golden oriole
(*Oriolus oriolus*)
Length: 10 in (25 cm)

The male is brightly colored to attract the paler female.

Eurasian golden oriole

The woven, grassy nest of the Eurasian golden oriole hangs below a forked branch like a hammock. This shy bird spends most of its time hidden high in the treetops feeding on insects and fruit. The female grasps food in her sharp, stout bill to feed to her young. During courtship the male flies after the female in a high-speed chase.

The female does most of the nest building and takes care of the young.

Common hoopoe

The common hoopoe is named after its loud call, which sounds like "hoo-poo-poo." It walks and runs over the ground, searching for worms and insects with its thin, curved bill. If a bird of prey flies overhead, the adult common hoopoe spreads its wings and tail flat against the ground and points its bill straight up, ready to attack the enemy. When it is excited, it raises the crest on its head.

Common hoopoe
(*Upupa epops*)
Length: 1 ft 1 in (32 cm)

The common hoopoe flaps its rounded black-and-white wings rather like a butterfly.

Garonne

Rhône

Douro

PYRENEES

ALPS

E U R O P E

CARPATHIAN MTS

Camargue
(See facing page)

Danube

BLACK SEA

APENNINES

COTO DE DOÑANA

SARDINIA

M E D I T E R R A N E A N   S E A

SICILY

A T L A S   M T S

Euphrates

N O R T H   A F R I C A

COMMON HOOPOE	WESTERN MARSH-HARRIER
EUROPEAN ROLLER	EURASIAN GOLDEN ORIOLE
NORTHERN SHOVELER	PURPLE HERON
PIED AVOCET	

0	250	500 km
0	150	300 miles

The Camargue

The salty marshes and shallow lakes of the Camargue nature reserve formed where the Rhône River meets the Mediterranean Sea. Despite people, houses, and industry all around and aircraft flying overhead, large numbers of wading birds and water birds live there, and even more pass through on their migration routes. Tens of thousands of swans, ducks, and geese visit the Camargue in winter from their breeding grounds in northern Europe and Siberia. The birds share the available food by feeding in different places and on different types of food: stilts feed in shallow water while little egrets and purple herons prefer deeper water; herons catch fish, while spoonbills, flamingos, and avocets feed on small water creatures.

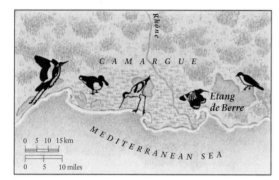

Western marsh-harrier

Western marsh-harrier
(*Circus aeruginosus*)
Length: up to 1 ft 9 in (54 cm)

Wings held in shallow V-shape to glide and soar over marshes

As it glides and flaps slowly over reed beds and grassland, the male western marsh-harrier searches for frogs, fish, small mammals, birds, and insects to eat. The female and her young stay in the nest, hidden among reeds and marsh plants. When the male brings food to the nest, the female flies up and catches it in mid-air. They also pass food in this way during courtship.

Males and females are both brown, but females have a light-colored crown, and adult males have some gray in their wings.

Purple heron
(*Ardea purpurea*)
Length: up to 3 ft (90 cm)

Very sharp, pointed bill to grab fish and frogs

Purple heron

The tall, slender purple heron has long toes to spread out its weight so that it can stalk over floating marsh plants without sinking in. Its long legs let it wade into deep water where it fishes for food with its long bill. The purple heron usually nests in small groups of up to 20 pairs. The nests are hidden among reeds or rushes in shallow water. When alarmed, the purple heron crouches with its bill pointing straight up. This pose, along with the stripes on its neck, make it hard to see among the reeds.

The heron is a shy bird, which makes it hard to see until it takes off, usually making a squawking noise.

Greater flamingos feed on plants and small animals in the shallow waters of the Camargue. Three-quarters of all the flamingo chicks in the Mediterranean region hatch here.

Pied avocet

The pointed, upturned bill of the pied avocet sweeps through water, or the soft mud beneath it, in search of food, such as worms and small water creatures. Avocets prefer to nest on islands, where their young are safer from attack. They usually nest in large colonies so they can join forces against predators.

Northern shoveler
(*Spatula clypeata*)
Length: 1 ft 10 in (56 cm)

The male is more colorful than the female.

Male

Big, shovellike bill for filtering food from water.

Northern shoveler

This bird, which spends its winters in the Mediterranean basin, gets its name from its shovel-shaped bill. At first, the chick has a normal bill, but this changes as it grows up. The adult shoveler sucks water into its wide bill and then pushes it out of the sides. Fine "combs" on the inside edges of the bill trap tiny floating animals and plants from the water as it flows over them.

Pied avocet
(*Recurvirostra avosetta*)
Length: 1 ft 6 in (45 cm)

Long legs and long bill for feeding in deep water

Coastal Areas

EUROPE'S JAGGED, IRREGULAR coastline provides many nesting places for seabirds. Millions come ashore in the summer to lay their eggs and raise their young. Although steep cliffs are dangerous for young birds, it is harder for predators to reach them. There is also safety in numbers—many seabirds crowd together in huge, noisy colonies made up of thousands of birds. Different species, such as guillemots, kittiwakes, gannets, and fulmars, may nest together on the same cliff. Each nests at a different level, sharing the small amount of space available. Unlike land birds, seabirds do not need a large feeding area or territory on land to gather food for their chicks. They feed mainly out at sea so they can nest close together on land.

Large, powerful wings for gliding and soaring

Long, strong legs for running and webbed feet for swimming

Great black-backed gull
(*Larus marinus*)
Length: up to 2 ft 7 in (79 cm)

Great black-backed gull

This large gull is a fierce hunter, taking a wide variety of prey, from fish and seabirds to rabbits. In the summer breeding season, it attacks seabird colonies on the coast, gulping down a chick in a single mouthful. At other times of year, it scavenges for scraps on trash piles inland and around fishing ports and beaches.

Little tern

Bustling colonies of little terns gather on sandy beaches in summer. Members of the colony may help each other dive-bomb enemies and drive them away. Young terns have to learn the best places to fish and how to dive headfirst into the water like their parents. Unfortunately, the number of these terns have decreased because of people disturbing them.

Little terns are graceful and agile in flight, sometimes hovering over the water.

Long, pointed wings beat quickly up and down.

Sharp, pointed bill for gripping fish

Little tern
(*Sternula albifrons*)
Length: 11 in (28 cm)

Common murre

The common murre, or guillemot, spends a lot of time far out at sea. To catch fish, it dives below the surface, beats its wings rapidly, and steers with its feet. It only comes to the coasts to breed, forming dense colonies on cliff ledges. The birds are usually packed so close together that they touch their neighbors. The common murre lays a single egg on bare rock, without a nest, so one parent always has to stay and protect the egg and chick and keep them warm while the other goes off to sea to feed.

European storm-petrel

The European storm-petrel is the smallest European seabird. Fluttering above the water, it picks up small fish and plankton from the surface. This petrel will often follow ships to feed on the scraps thrown overboard and may shelter near ships during storms. It nests in colonies, mostly on isolated islands because it cannot defend itself easily.

Common murre
(*Uria aalge*)
Length: 1 ft 5 in (43 cm)

Streamlined shape helps the bird move fast through the water.

Narrow, pointed bill for seizing fish

Slim, hooked bill

As it feeds, the bird's legs dangle down so it looks as if it is "walking" on water.

European storm-petrel
(*Hydrobates pelagicus*)
Length: 7 in (18 cm)

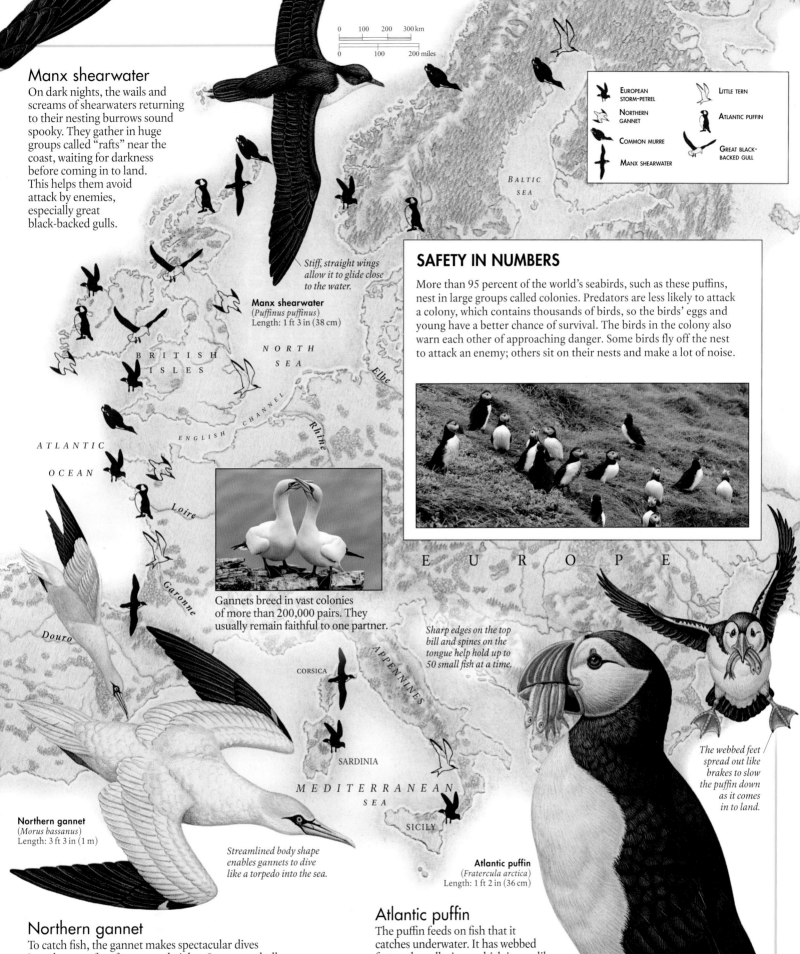

Manx shearwater

On dark nights, the wails and screams of shearwaters returning to their nesting burrows sound spooky. They gather in huge groups called "rafts" near the coast, waiting for darkness before coming in to land. This helps them avoid attack by enemies, especially great black-backed gulls.

Stiff, straight wings allow it to glide close to the water.

Manx shearwater
(*Puffinus puffinus*)
Length: 1 ft 3 in (38 cm)

0 100 200 300 km

0 100 200 miles

EUROPEAN
STORM-PETREL

NORTHERN
GANNET

COMMON MURRE

MANX SHEARWATER

LITTLE TERN

ATLANTIC PUFFIN

GREAT BLACK-
BACKED GULL

BALTIC
SEA

NORTH
SEA

BRITISH
ISLES

Elbe

ENGLISH CHANNEL

Rhine

ATLANTIC
OCEAN

Loire

Garonne

Douro

SAFETY IN NUMBERS

More than 95 percent of the world's seabirds, such as these puffins, nest in large groups called colonies. Predators are less likely to attack a colony, which contains thousands of birds, so the birds' eggs and young have a better chance of survival. The birds in the colony also warn each other of approaching danger. Some birds fly off the nest to attack an enemy; others sit on their nests and make a lot of noise.

E U R O P E

Gannets breed in vast colonies of more than 200,000 pairs. They usually remain faithful to one partner.

Sharp edges on the top bill and spines on the tongue help hold up to 50 small fish at a time.

CORSICA

APPENNINES

SARDINIA

MEDITERRANEAN
SEA

SICILY

The webbed feet spread out like brakes to slow the puffin down as it comes in to land.

Northern gannet
(*Morus bassanus*)
Length: 3 ft 3 in (1 m)

Streamlined body shape enables gannets to dive like a torpedo into the sea.

Atlantic puffin
(*Fratercula arctica*)
Length: 1 ft 2 in (36 cm)

Northern gannet

To catch fish, the gannet makes spectacular dives into the sea, often from great heights. Its strong skull helps it withstand the impact of hitting the water and its nostrils can be closed off underwater. It uses its stout bill to grasp prey, such as fish and squid, and drag it to the surface. During the breeding season, the birds nest very close together. After about 14 weeks on the nest, the chicks head out to sea. They do not develop their final adult colors for five to six years.

Atlantic puffin

The puffin feeds on fish that it catches underwater. It has webbed feet and small wings, which it uses like fins to propel itself through the water. In the breeding season, the puffin develops a larger, more powerful bill to attract a mate. The bill is also used to dig a nesting burrow in a grassy cliff-top. When it has grown its feathers, the young puffin leaves its burrow under cover of darkness to avoid predators.

AFRICA

AFRICA IS THE SECOND LARGEST continent in the world. It is nearly three times as big as Europe, but about the same number of people live there. It was cut off from the other continents for millions of years and many of its birds—the ostrich, the shoebill, the secretary bird, as well as turacos, mousebirds, wood hoopoes, and helmet shrikes—are not found anywhere else in the world.

Africa is mainly a dry continent with large areas of desert and dry grassland. As a result, it has many land birds, especially seed-eaters.

Despite its vast area of inhospitable terrain, the Sahara desert is on the migration route for billions of birds that make this journey every year to escape the European winter. The desert is spreading due to climate change and increased periods of drought. People have also caused the desert to spread at the edges by grazing too many animals there and reducing the vegetation cover. Africa's rich and varied bird life is also threatened by people cutting down forests, draining marshes and swamps, and building farms and cities.

Climate and landscape

Most of Africa has a hot climate, with large areas that receive very little rain, especially the Sahara desert in the north and the Namib and Kalahari deserts in the southwest. The wettest areas are near the Equator in the center of the continent. Unlike other continents, Africa has few mountain chains. Generally, there are high, flat plains sometimes broken by a single mountain, such as Mount Kilimanjaro in Tanzania, East Africa.

Africa on the move

Africa has not always been in the position it is in today. Like all the other continents, it has gradually shifted around Earth due to movements in the crust. Africa was once attached to the other continents, but over millions of years, it has drifted away. African birds evolved into many unique species because they could not mix with birds from other continents.

About 130 million years ago, Africa started to split away from the other continents and became a single continent. At that time Madagascar was still joined to mainland Africa. Later, it drifted away to become an island, so the bird life there developed separately from that in mainland Africa.

In the last 100 million years, Africa has drifted toward Europe to its position on today's globe.

AMAZING BIRDS OF AFRICA

Red-billed quelea
(*Quelea quelea*)

Most abundant bird
There are more red-billed queleas in the world than any other bird. Feeding flocks may contain millions of birds and colonies and can have up to 10 million nests.

Longest toes
Relative to its body size, the African jacana has the longest toes: up to 3 in (8 cm) long.

Highest flier
A Rüppell's griffon vulture collided with a plane when flying over the coast of West Africa at an altitude of 36,988 ft (11,274 m). This is the highest altitude a bird has ever been seen at.

Broadest bill
The shoebill or whale-headed stork has the broadest bill of any bird—5 in (12 cm) wide.

Largest bird
The African common ostrich is the world's largest and tallest bird. Males can be up to 9 ft (2 m 70 cm) tall and weigh as much as 344 lb (156 kg). The ostrich also lays the largest eggs. A person can stand on one of these eggs without breaking it.

Common ostrich
(*Struthio camelus*)

ARABIAN
PENINSULA

RED SEA

Nile

Lake Chad

TIBESTI MTS

HOGGAR MTS

EUROPE

MEDITERRANEAN SEA

ATLAS MTS

A F R I C A

S A H A R A   D E S E R T

Niger

FACTS ABOUT AFRICA

Number of birds
More than 2,500 species of bird live in Africa. Kenya has a particularly rich bird life, with more than 1,000 different species.

Deep lake
Lake Tanganyika is 4,708 ft (1,435 m) deep and is the second deepest lake in the world. Africa's largest lake is Lake Victoria, but this is only 266 ft (81 m) deep.

Longest river
The Nile is 4,145 miles (6,670 km) long and is the world's longest river.

Spectacular waterfall
The Victoria Falls on the Zambezi River drop 355 ft (108 m) over a ledge 5,580 ft (1,700 m) wide.

Biggest desert
The Sahara is the biggest desert in the world—it covers an area of about 3.5 million sq miles (9 million sq km). The world's highest sand dunes occur in the Sahara. They can be up to 1,410 ft (430 m) high.

Colossal crack
The Great Rift Valley is about 4,000 miles (6,400 km) long and in some parts it is 22–37 miles (35–60 km) wide. It formed about 25 million years ago when land slipped down between huge cracks, probably due to movements of Earth's crust.

Typical birds
Here are just a few examples of typical birds from the most important habitats of Africa. These range from hot, dry deserts and open grasslands to warm, humid rainforests and rivers, lakes, and swamps.

Savanna
There are only two species of oxpecker in the world and they both live on the African savanna. Oxpeckers live on insects, which they take from the skin of grazing animals, such as this giraffe.

Deserts
Most birds find it hard to survive in a dry desert habitat, but the sandgrouse can live well on a diet of dry seeds and fly long distances to water holes.

Islands
The cuckoo roller is one of many unique bird families that live only on the island of Madagascar. Others include the ground rollers, asities, and vanga shrikes.

Rainforests
This pitta is a common bird of the rainforests. African rainforests used to be more widespread, but have shrunk as the climate became drier and as people cut down the trees.

Mountains
Birds of prey, such as this Verreaux's eagle, thrive in the African mountains where they can soar aloft rising air currents and see their prey running on the bare ground below.

Lakes and rivers
Kingfishers, such as this pied kingfisher, are a common sight around African lakes and rivers, which are rich in food and nesting places.

Marshes and swamps
Large numbers of fish-eating birds, such as this goliath heron, live and feed in vast tropical swamplands such as the Okavango Delta in southern Africa.

These storm clouds signal the start of the rainy season on the Tanzanian grasslands. Some African birds migrate within Africa, following the rains.

ETHIOPIAN HIGHLANDS

Congo

INDIAN OCEAN

Lake Victoria

Lake Tanganyika

GREAT RIFT VALLEY

Lake Malawi

Zambezi

MADAGASCAR

Hyrax

KALAHARI DESERT

NAMIB DESERT

ATLANTIC OCEAN

Forests and Mountains

STRETCHING ACROSS the center of Africa is the second largest area of rainforest in the world. It grows in the tropical regions around the Equator, where the climate is hot and wet all year round. A variety of birds, such as hornbills, turacos, and pittas, thrive in this rich environment, where there are plenty of leaves, fruits, and insects to eat and trees and bushes to nest in. There are also areas of rainforest growing on the lower slopes of the mountains in East Africa. On the higher slopes is a cold, misty world of grasses and giant plants, which is home to birds such as eagles and sunbirds.

The island of Madagascar off the east coast of Africa has areas of both mountain and rainforest, as well as deserts and grasslands. Many unique animals have evolved in this varied environment. These include several families of birds that are not found anywhere else in the world.

Sunbirds often feed on giant lobelia.

Red-tufted sunbird
(*Nectarinia johnstoni*)
Length: 11 in (27 cm)
Male's tail: up to 8 in (20 cm)

Both males and females puff out these red tufts to attract a mate.

Male's chest feathers turn green during the breeding season; at other times, they are brown.

Red-tufted sunbird

This large mountain sunbird often perches on flowers to probe for nectar with its long, thin, curved bill. It has strong feet and sharp claws for gripping slippery leaves. It also eats a lot of insects, holding them in the jagged edges near the tip of its bill. As it feeds, it helps spread pollen from flower to flower. It has little flaps over its nostrils to stop pollen dust from getting up its nose.

Green wood hoopoe

These birds move around in a noisy family group, probing tree trunks and branches for insect grubs with their long, curved bills. Several times each hour, the birds perform a cackling display, which helps keep the main group together. Up to ten green wood hoopoes help each set of parents gather food and defend the eggs and chicks. When the chicks grow up, they may become "helpers" for the adults who cared for them.

During the cackling display, the birds face each other, rocking to and fro and bowing low.

Strong, hooked bill is used mainly for catching insects but the helmet vanga will also eat frogs and small reptiles, such as this chameleon.

Helmet vanga
(*Euryceros prevostii*)
Length: 1 ft (31 cm)

Helmet vanga

This bird belongs to a group of birds called the vangas, found only on the island of Madagascar. There are 14 species of vanga on the island. These probably evolved over millions of years from a single ancestor, which crossed over from the African mainland. Each of the species lives in a different habitat, so that there are enough nest sites and food to go round.

Tail is raised high in the air when the bird displays.

Green wood hoopoe
(*Phoeniculus purpureus*)
Length: 1 ft 4 in (40 cm)

Legend:
- Great blue turaco
- Helmet vanga
- African pitta
- Congo peafowl
- Trumpeter hornbill
- Green wood hoopoe
- Red-tufted sunbird

AFRICA

Senegal · *Niger* · *White Nile* · *Blue Nile* · *RED SEA*

Congo · *GREAT RIFT VALLEY* · *Lake Victoria* · *Lake Tanganyika*

ATLANTIC OCEAN · *Congo* · *Kasai* · *Lake Malawi* · *Zambezi*

Lake Kariba · *KALAHARI DESERT* · *Limpopo*

Orange River · *DRAKENSBERG MTS* · *INDIAN OCEAN*

MOZAMBIQUE CHANNEL · *MADAGASCAR*

| 0 | 250 | 500 | 750 km |
| 0 | | 250 | 500 miles |

Giant groundsels grow high on the African mountains. Sunbirds nest among their cabbage-like leaves.

The casque on top of the bill is light and spongy inside. Males, like this bird, have larger casques than females.

Large, curved bill enables the bird to reach fruit in the trees and to toss it into its mouth.

Trumpeter hornbill
(*Bycanistes bucinator*)
Length: 1 ft 10 in (55 cm)

Great blue turaco
(*Corythaeola cristata*)
Length: 2 ft 6½ in (75 cm)

Great blue turaco

Groups of up to 12 great blue turacos run and climb through the treetops. They feed on fruits, including berries that are poisonous to humans. The nest is a flimsy platform of twigs built in a tall tree. When very young, chicks scramble around the nest using tiny claws on their wings to keep their balance. After about four weeks, they leave the nest for good.

Trumpeter hornbill

The loud, wailing call of the trumpeter hornbill sounds like a child crying. Most hornbills have very unusual nesting habits. A pair build a round nest inside a hole in a tree then seal the opening, leaving the female inside. The male passes food to her through a narrow slit. This temporary prison protects her and her chicks from predators.

Only males have this tuft of white bristles.

African pitta
(*Pitta angolensis*)
Length: 8 in (20 cm)

African pitta

The shy African pitta hops through dense undergrowth on the rainforest floor searching for slugs and insects. Although it is brightly colored, it blends in surprisingly well with the leafy forest background. To threaten enemies, it crouches down with its wings spread and its bill pointing upward.

Congo peafowl

This unusual bird is the only true African pheasant—all the others originally came from Asia. Unlike other pheasants, such as the common peafowl (peacock), the Congo peafowl has a short tail. It lives on the rainforest floor, feeding on fruits and insects.

Both males and females have bright, shiny feathers.

Congo peafowl
(*Afropavo congensis*)
Length: 2 ft 3 in (70 cm)

The Savanna

THE DRY, GRASSY PLAINS of the savanna provide food for a variety of seed- and insect-eating birds. Some of these birds depend on the mammals of the grasslands for their food. Oxpeckers, for instance, cling to giraffes, zebras, rhinos, and other animals with their sharp claws and snap up their ticks and other blood-sucking parasites. Vultures and marabou storks help clean up the carcasses left by lions and other big cats.

In some parts of the savanna, trees, such as the flat-topped acacias, can be used as nest sites by birds such as weavers, starlings, or rollers. Other small birds hide their nests on the ground. The savanna has a wet season and a dry season. Birds tend to raise their young after the rains, when the grasses are green and lush and there is plenty of food. Savanna bird life is increasingly threatened by people who live on and farm the remaining grasslands.

Martial eagle

This is the largest and most powerful eagle in Africa. A female may have a wingspan of 7 ft 7 in (2 m 30 cm). This eagle either swoops down from great heights at high speed to attack its prey or lies in wait to ambush prey from a branch. The martial eagle builds its nest in tall trees. Females usually lay just one egg.

Hooked bill for tearing flesh from food

Martial eagle
(*Polemaetus bellicosus*)
Length: 3 ft 2 in (96 cm)

Very strong, curved talons to kill prey

| 0 | 400 | 800 | 1,200 km |
| 0 | 400 | | 800 miles |

ATLAS MTS

SAHARA

Niger

Common ostrich
(*Struthio camelus*)
Length: 9 ft 1 in (2 m 75 cm)
Height: up to 9 ft 2 in (2 m 80 cm)

Secretary bird

This bird was so named because its crest makes it look like an old-fashioned secretary with a quill pen stuck behind its ear. It feeds on small mammals, insects, and some birds and their eggs. It can also kill snakes. The secretary bird snaps up small animals in its sharp bill but kills larger ones by stamping on them. During courtship, the birds fly up high making strange calls. The nest is a platform of sticks, which is built in the top of a tree.

Secretary bird
(*Sagittarius serpentarius*)
Length: 5 ft (1 m 50 cm)

The head crest is often raised while the bird is hunting.

Ostriches are the only birds with two toes on each foot.

Strong legs and toes, enable it to run at up to 43 mph (70 kph).

Common ostrich

The ostrich is the largest and tallest bird alive today. It strides effortlessly across the savanna searching for leaves, seeds, and insects with its sharp eyes. The male makes a nest by scraping a hollow in the ground. Several females lay their eggs in one nest.

Long legs enable it to walk easily through the tall grasses.

VULTURES

Soaring above the African grasslands, white-backed vultures like these look out for dead animals to feed on. Their bare heads and necks allow them to feed without getting any feathers dirty. After a meal, vultures clean their feathers well to keep them in good condition for flying.

Village weaver

Village weavers live in flocks and build their nests together so that they are safer from attack. There may be as many as 100 nests in one tree. The male builds the nest from strips of grass which he weaves into a round ball. He starts by building a swing to perch on, then makes a ring shape and finally a round ball. To attract a female, a male hangs upside down from the nest, flicking his wings. If a female likes the nest, she lays her eggs there and raises her young by herself.

These village weavers' nests are at the tips of branches where predators such as snakes cannot reach them.

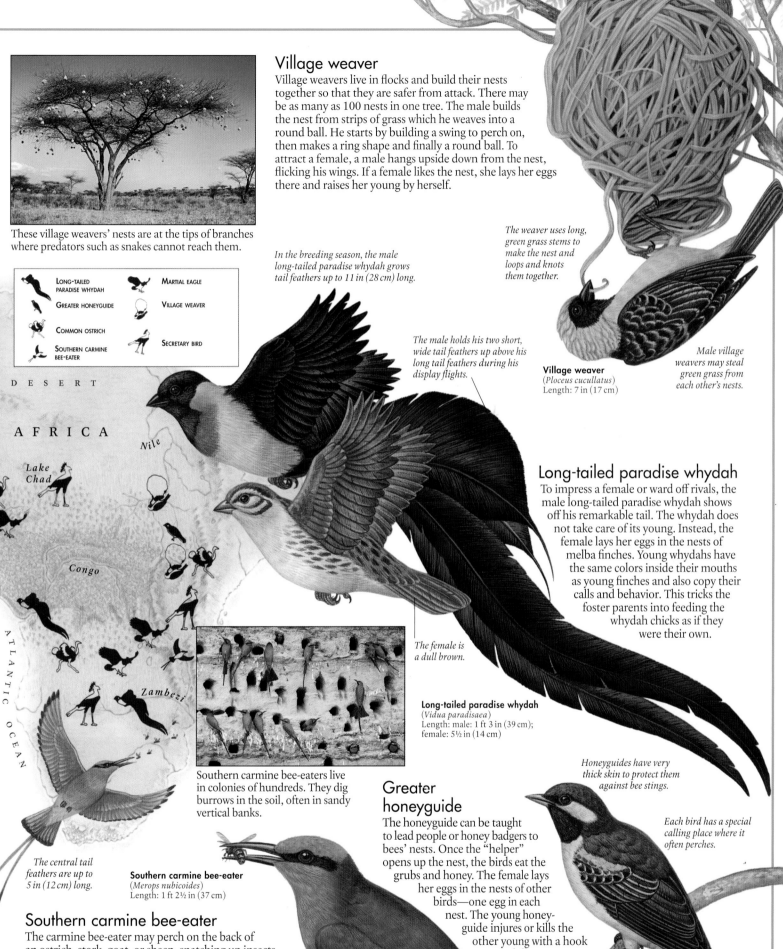

The weaver uses long, green grass stems to make the nest and loops and knots them together.

In the breeding season, the male long-tailed paradise whydah grows tail feathers up to 11 in (28 cm) long.

The male holds his two short, wide tail feathers up above his long tail feathers during his display flights.

Village weaver
(Ploceus cucullatus)
Length: 7 in (17 cm)

Male village weavers may steal green grass from each other's nests.

LONG-TAILED PARADISE WHYDAH
GREATER HONEYGUIDE
COMMON OSTRICH
SOUTHERN CARMINE BEE-EATER
MARTIAL EAGLE
VILLAGE WEAVER
SECRETARY BIRD

DESERT

AFRICA

Nile

Lake Chad

ATLANTIC OCEAN

Congo

Zambezi

Long-tailed paradise whydah

To impress a female or ward off rivals, the male long-tailed paradise whydah shows off his remarkable tail. The whydah does not take care of its young. Instead, the female lays her eggs in the nests of melba finches. Young whydahs have the same colors inside their mouths as young finches and also copy their calls and behavior. This tricks the foster parents into feeding the whydah chicks as if they were their own.

The female is a dull brown.

Long-tailed paradise whydah
(Vidua paradisaea)
Length: male: 1 ft 3 in (39 cm);
female: 5½ in (14 cm)

Southern carmine bee-eaters live in colonies of hundreds. They dig burrows in the soil, often in sandy vertical banks.

The central tail feathers are up to 5 in (12 cm) long.

Southern carmine bee-eater
(Merops nubicoides)
Length: 1 ft 2½ in (37 cm)

Greater honeyguide

The honeyguide can be taught to lead people or honey badgers to bees' nests. Once the "helper" opens up the nest, the birds eat the grubs and honey. The female lays her eggs in the nests of other birds—one egg in each nest. The young honeyguide injures or kills the other young with a hook on its bill.

Honeyguides have very thick skin to protect them against bee stings.

Each bird has a special calling place where it often perches.

Southern carmine bee-eater

The carmine bee-eater may perch on the back of an ostrich, stork, goat, or sheep, snatching up insects disturbed by its feet. It also gathers near grass fires where it eats up the insects trying to escape from the flames. The bee-eater specializes in eating stinging insects. To get rid of the sting, it holds the insect tightly in its bill and beats and rubs it against a perch. Then it swallows the insect whole.

Greater honeyguide
(Indicator indicator)
Length: 8 in (20 cm)

Rivers, Lakes, and Swamps

AFRICA'S FRESHWATER HABITATS include great rivers such as the Nile and the Niger as well as vast swamps such as the Sudd and the Okavango Delta. These swamps, and the marshes that surround the great rivers, teem with life, especially fish. Large numbers of fish-eating birds live there, including herons, egrets, ibises, storks, and pelicans. Reeds and rafts of lilies growing in the warm, shallow waters also provide nest sites and safe places to feed.

In the east of Africa lies the long, narrow Great Rift Valley. It has formed where a section of Earth's crust is slowly splitting, causing the land in between to sink. On the flat valley floor are many spectacular lakes. Birds from Europe and Asia use African lakes and swamps as resting places when they migrate across the continent.

African fish eagle
(*Haliaeetus vocifer*)
Length: 2 ft 6½ in (75 cm)

Courting males and females show off their flying skills—they try to grab each other's talons as they tumble downward through the air.

African fish eagle
This bird spends much of its time perched in tall trees near water. From time to time, it swoops down to snatch fish from the surface in its powerful claws. Sometimes it plunges underwater feet first and then rises up, lifting the fish clear out of the water.

BLACK HERON		AFRICAN FISH EAGLE	
HAMERKOP		PEL'S FISHING OWL	
AFRICAN JACANA		SHOEBILL	
LESSER FLAMINGO			

Pel's fishing owl
(*Scotopelia peli*)
Length: 2 ft (61 cm)

Large eyes help the owl to see well in the dark.

Pel's fishing owl
During the day, Pel's fishing owl hides away in trees near rivers and swamps. At night, it swoops low over the water and catches fish in its powerful feet. Its legs and feet are bare so it has no feathers that could trail in the water. Unlike other owls, fishing owls do not have fringed feathers and soft plumage for silent flight as they do not need to fly quietly to sneak up on fish.

Feet have small spikes underneath to grip slippery fish or frogs.

AFRICA

ATLANTIC OCEAN

Niger

Lake Volta

Congo

Congo

Congo

SUDD

White Nile

Lake Tana

GULF OF ADEN

Lake Turkana

Lake Victoria

GREAT RIFT VALLEY

INDIAN OCEAN

Lake Tanganyika

Lake Malawi

Zambezi

OKAVANGO DELTA

KALAHARI DESERT

Limpopo

Orange River

Millions of flamingos flock to Rift Valley lakes, such as Lake Nakuru, to feed on the microscopic plants and animals growing there.

0	300	600	900 km

0	300	600 miles

Black heron

The black heron, or black egret, fishes for food in an unusual way. It spreads its wings out around its head to shade the water. The reason for this could be that the shaded area cuts out reflections on the surface of the water and makes it easier for the bird to see fish. Another explanation is that fish may swim into the dark patch thinking it is a safe shelter. When the heron spots a fish, it jabs its bill quickly into the water.

The bird makes an "umbrella" over the water with its wings for 2–3 seconds at a time by day or night.

Hamerkop

Hamerkop
(*Scopus umbretta*)
Length: 1 ft 10 in (56 cm)

This bird is named after its hammer-shaped head. It builds a huge, roofed nest of twigs, grass, and mud, usually high in a tree near water. The nest is decorated with feathers, bones, snakeskins, and trash that people have thrown away. It is strong enough for a person to stand on the roof without falling in. Chicks are safe inside its thick walls while the parents find food.

Short tail and large wings for gliding and soaring easily.

Each nest takes 1–6 months to build, but hamerkops often build several nests each year—no one knows why.

Toes are partly webbed.

Huge head to support the massive bill.

Large eyes help see fish and other prey in the water.

Black heron
(*Egretta ardesiaca*)
Length: up to 2 ft 2 in (66 cm)

Long, thin bill to catch prey.

Hook at tip of bill helps grab hold of wet, slippery food.

Shoebill
(*Balaeniceps rex*)
Length: 4 ft (1 m 20 cm)

Lesser flamingo

Thousands of these flamingos flock to African lakes to nest and feed on tiny water plants. To make sure the chicks get enough food, the parents produce a kind of rich "milk" in their crop—a pouch in the wall of the gut. The milk is bright red because it is dyed by pink pigment from the algae they eat. Their feathers are pink for the same reason.

Shoebill

This bird is named for its extraordinary shoe-shaped bill. The huge bill helps the bird catch and hold its favorite food—lungfish. It also eats young crocodiles, turtles, frogs, and snakes. Parents sometimes collect water in their bills and pour it over their chicks in hot weather to keep them cool.

Lesser flamingo
(*Phoeniconaias minor*)
Length: 3 ft (90 cm)

African jacana
(*Actophilornis africanus*)
Length: 1 ft (31 cm)

Chicks make begging calls when they are hungry.

Long toes and claws spread out the bird's weight so it can walk on floating plants without sinking.

African jacana

These birds are also called lily-trotters. They run over floating plants pecking at the water and leaves to collect food. The male builds the nest, sits on the eggs, and takes care of the chicks, which is very rare for a male bird—female birds usually raise the young, often on their own.

ASIA

ASIA IS THE LARGEST CONTINENT on the planet. Much of northern, central, and southwest Asia has a cold, dry climate, with harsh deserts, dry grasslands, and frozen forests where few birds can survive. Many birds are forced to migrate south during colder seasons. The warm, rainy, tropical lands of Southeast Asia are, however, home to a spectacular variety of birds including pheasants, babblers, flycatchers, warblers, and thrushes. Some birds, such as the golden-fronted leafbird, the great argus pheasant, and the rhinoceros hornbill are not found anywhere else in the world.

To the west, Asia is attached to Europe and Africa and some of the birds are the same as, or similar to, birds in these continents. To the south, the islands of Southeast Asia form a series of stepping stones along which birds can move to and from New Guinea and Australia.

About half the world's population lives in Asia. They have made major changes to the land and plant life across the continent. Birds are increasingly threatened by the spread of cities and by forest destruction. Unless birds can adapt to an urban lifestyle, they have nowhere to live when their natural homes are destroyed.

India on the move

Over millions of years, continental drift has caused India to move into different positions on the globe.

About 200 million years ago, India was attached to Africa, Australia, and Antarctica. But it split away on its own and slowly began to drift northward toward Asia (right).

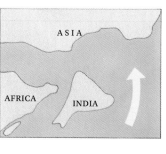

About 60–40 million years ago, India crashed into Asia, pushing up land from under the sea to create the gigantic folds of land that form the Himalayan Mountains. India is still pushing into Asia at a rate of about 0.6 miles (1 km) every 100,000 years.

Climate and landscape

The great Asian mountain chains, such as the Karakoram, Pamirs, and Himalayas, cut across Asia from east to west, separating the warmer, wetter lands of India and Southeast Asia from the cooler, drier lands of central Asia. Southeast Asia consists mainly of thousands of islands, many of which were formed by volcanoes erupting through the seabed.

Many Southeast Asian islands, such as these in Indonesia, have a monsoon climate, with heavy rain in summer and cooler, drier winters. Seasons are altered by strong winds.

AMAZING BIRDS OF ASIA

Loud woodpecker
This enormous woodpecker can be heard hammering at tree trunks from up to 1.12 miles (1.8 km) away.

Black woodpecker
(*Dryocopus martius*)

Heaviest head
The helmeted hornbill has a solid ivory casque on top of its bill, giving it the heaviest bill of any bird.

Biggest tail
The crested argus pheasant has the longest feathers and the longest and largest tail in the world. A male's tail feathers can reach 5 ft 8 in (1 m 73 cm) long and 5 in (13 cm) wide.

Quick chicks
The chicks of the Cabot's tragopan are some of the quickest to fly after hatching. They grow all their flight feathers within 24 hours of hatching and can flutter up into the trees immediately.

Heaviest flier
The Kori bustard is the world's heaviest flying bird. Males can weigh up to 42 lb (19 kg).

Kori bustard
(*Ardeotis kori*)

FACTS ABOUT ASIA

Highest mountains
The Himalayas are the world's highest mountain range and contain the highest point on Earth—Mount Everest—which reaches 29,028 ft (8,848 m).

Number of birds
About 2,600 species of bird live in tropical Asia, from India in the west to China in the east and the Indonesian islands of Sumatra and Java in the south. More than 600 species breed in the Philippines alone.

Biggest forest
The conifer forests of northern Asia, called the taiga, cover more than 4½ million sq miles (12 million sq km) from Scandinavia in the west to the coast of the Pacific Ocean in the east. The taiga is the largest forest in the world.

Most volcanoes
Java in Indonesia has about 50 volcanoes. Mount Bromo (below) is the biggest of them. Volcanic soils cover about 16 percent of Japan.

Largest delta
The delta of the Ganges and Brahmaputra rivers in India covers an area of 23,000 sq miles (60,000 sq km).

Deepest lake on Earth
Lake Baikal in Siberia is the largest lake in Asia. It is 5,317 ft (1,637 m) deep and contains one-fifth of all the fresh water on Earth.

Highest rainfall
Cherrapunji in India has the highest rainfall in the world—425 in (10,800 mm) a year.

Typical birds

Here are just a few examples of typical birds from the most important habitats of Asia. You can find out more about typical birds and their habitats on the next few pages.

Rainforest
This orange-breasted trogon is one of 12 species of trogon that live in Southeast Asian rainforests. Other typical rainforest birds of the region include hornbills, barbets, broadbills, pittas, and sunbirds.

Mountains
Birds such as this satyr tragopan live high on mountains in summer and move lower down in winter. Asian mountains provide a range of habitats very close together, from tropical forests and deciduous and conifer woods to grasslands and rocky, snowy peaks.

Conifer forest
Crossbills are common birds in the vast taiga forest of northern Asia. Other forest birds include jays, waxwings, owls, tits, woodpeckers, nutcrackers, and grouse.

Desert and scrubland
Shrikes, larks, chats, and sandgrouse, feed on insects and seeds in this habitat. This long-tailed shrike is an aggressive predator that feeds on frogs as well as other birds.

Rivers, lakes, and swamps
The Asian openbill stork shares its watery habitat with other storks, herons, rails, cranes, spoonbills, ibises, ducks, geese, and swans.

Woodlands
More than 50 pheasant species, including this common peafowl, live in the forests of tropical mainland Asia and the Southeast Asian islands. Many pheasants are endangered by forest destruction.

Urban
This house crow thrives near people's fields, houses, and gardens, together with birds such as pigeons, starlings, mynahs, parakeets, and sparrows.

BERING SEA

Lena

SEA OF OKHOTSK

Lake Baikal

HOKKAIDO

SEA OF JAPAN

HONSHU

J A P A N

KOREA

SHIKOKU

RYUSHU

Yellow River

EAST CHINA SEA

PACIFIC OCEAN

A S I A

Yangtze

C H I N A

TAIWAN

PHILIPPINES

Mekong

GULF OF THAILAND

ANDAMAN SEA

SOUTH CHINA SEA

NEW GUINEA

BORNEO

SULAWESI

SUMATRA

I N D O N E S I A

JAVA

AUSTRALIA

The Himalayas

FROM THE FROZEN snow-covered peaks down to the hot forests on the lower slopes, the huge Himalayan Mountains provide a wide range of habitats for birds. On the bleakest rocky slopes, the bitterly cold weather causes the death of many animals, so bearded vultures, ravens, and other birds that eat dead animals have a steady food supply. In the warmer summer months, flower meadows further down the slopes are alive with buzzing insects. Accentors and redstarts eagerly snap these up, while the pigeons and partridges that also feed in these high meadows prefer to eat shoots and bulbs.

Many birds spend the summer feeding and nesting high up the mountains, but fly down to the sheltered forests in the foothills for the winter. These forests are rich in fruits and seeds and teem with mynahs, babblers, and parakeets. Many Himalayan forests have been cut down, and with fewer trees to soak up the rain and keep the soil firmly in place, water pours down the mountains causing serious floods.

Bar-headed goose

These geese breed in central Asia and migrate over the Himalayas—flying at record-breaking altitudes—to spend the winter in India. They rest by day near rivers and lakes. At night they graze in fields of crops, so farmers often shoot them. As they fly from one feeding ground to another, they make a wild, honking sound.

Bar-headed goose
(*Anser indicus*)
Length: 2 ft 6 in (76 cm)

Flocks of geese fly in formation so that the wind flows past them more easily and doesn't hold them back.

Bearded vulture
(*Gypaetus barbatus*)
Length: 4 ft (1 m 20 cm)
Wingspan: up to 9 ft 2 in (2 m 80 cm)

Bearded vulture

The acrobatic bearded vulture, or lammergeier, glides and soars over the high mountain slopes, searching for skeletons that have been picked clean by its cousin, the griffon vulture. The bearded vulture feeds on the marrow inside bones. The bird flies up to great heights and drops the bones on to rocks to smash them apart. It may drop one bone up to 50 times before breaking it. A bearded vulture will return to the same site year after year to crack open bones, and occasionally tortoise shells, in this way.

Long, thin tongue shaped like a garden trowel for scooping marrow from bones.

Stiff, black feathers hang down like a beard.

Wallcreeper

The nimble wallcreeper climbs up sheer walls of rock, probing for insects with its curved, pointed bill. It often spreads out its wings to keep itself propped up while it searches. In summer, it moves high up the mountains, but in winter, it moves down to the shelter of the lower slopes.

Wallcreeper
(*Tichodroma muraria*)
Length: 7 in (17 cm)

Flutters its wings like a butterfly, so it is also known as the "butterfly bird."

The male has a black throat in summer.

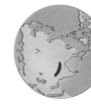

Himalayan Monal	**Himalayan Bulbul**	**Common Hill Mynah**	
Bar-headed Goose	**Bearded Vulture**	**Wallcreeper**	
Himalayan Snowcock			

HINDU KUSH

Indus

HIMALAYAS

INDIA

Brahmaputra

Ganges

Indus

Short, strong legs for mountain climbing

Himalayan monal
(*Lophophorus impejanus*)
Length: 2 ft 4 in (72 cm)

A male common peafowl displays his magnificent feathers. Many other spectacular pheasants live in the forests of the Himalayas.

Common hill mynah
(*Gracula religiosa*)
Length: 1 ft (31 cm)

Male

Female

Female's brown feathers help camouflage her on the nest.

Himalayan monal

This pheasant lives in the forests and meadows of the Himalayas, moving up and down the mountains with the seasons. It uses its powerful, curved bill as a digging tool to uncover roots, bulbs, and insect grubs. To display to a female, the male raises his crest, fluffs out his shiny neck feathers, fans his tail, and droops his wings.

Bright yellow face wattles (folds of skin) stand out against the glossy black feathers.

Common hill mynah

The noisy hill mynah lives in the tops of forest trees on the lower mountain slopes, feeding mainly on fruits and nectar. It makes a wide variety of whistling calls and is a brilliant mimic of the human voice. People have taken many of these birds from the wild to be kept as "talking" pets.

This species of bulbul has a long crest.

Himalayan bulbul

This lively bulbul lives as high up as 7,000 ft (2,100 m) in the Himalayas. It often perches on the tops of bushes, bowing, flicking its tail, and calling loudly. The Himalayan bulbul is not frightened of people. It is an inquisitive bird that lives near villages and towns and sometimes goes right inside houses to steal food.

Himalayan bulbul
(*Pycnonotus leucotis*)
Length: 7½ in (19 cm)

Short wings and a long tail are characteristic of bulbuls.

Flocks of birds, such as these snow pigeons, fly at very high altitudes across the peaks of the Himalayas.

Himalayan snowcock

The mottled colors of the Himalayan snowcock blend in well with the rocks and snow on the high mountain slopes. It eats all sorts of plant material, including roots, tubers, berries, shoots, and seeds, but it often has to search large areas to find enough to eat. In the breeding season, males make whistling calls to impress females.

Himalayan snowcock
(*Tetraogallus himalayensis*)
Length: 2 ft 4 in (72 cm)

BAY OF BENGAL

INDIAN OCEAN

Irrawaddy

Narmada

Godavari

EASTERN GHATS

DECCAN PLATEAU

WESTERN GHATS

GULF OF KHAMBHAT

450 km
300
150
0

300 miles
150
0

Southeast Asia

BETWEEN THE SOUTHERN EDGE of mainland Asia and northern Australasia is an area of shallow seas dotted with thousands of islands. On the islands nearest Australia and New Guinea, Asian and Australasian birds mix together. On more remote islands, such as the Philippines, many unique birds have developed away from contact with other species.

The rich volcanic soils and hot, humid climate in this region have encouraged the growth of lush rainforests, where a huge variety of birds live. Great numbers of birds often gather on the fruit-bearing trees, but they are well camouflaged and hard to see in the depths of the forest. Many people live in this region and much of the original rainforest has been cleared to make way for villages, towns, mines, and farms. This leaves the birds with fewer places to live and threatens the survival of many species.

Deep, hooked bill for ripping open prey.

Greater Philippine eagle
(*Pithecophaga jefferyi*)
Length: 3 ft 3 in (1 m)

Greater Philippine eagle

This fierce eagle glides over the treetops or swoops down from a perch to catch its prey. It hunts monkeys and flying lemurs (called colugos), as well as small deer and large birds such as hornbills. The Greater philippine eagle is one of the rarest birds of prey in the world because of the destruction of its forest home. Possibly only a few hundred of them survive in the wild.

Flying lemurs (colugos) are a favorite food.

Two very long feathers in the middle of the tail.

The male fans out his stunning wing feathers to impress a female.

HORNBILLS

Hornbills are named after the strange, hornlike growth, called a casque, which many of them have on top of their bills. It is made of a thin layer of skin and bone over a light "honeycomb" structure. No one really knows what the casque is for. It may help one hornbill tell the sex and age of another, or it may make the bird's call louder.

Great argus

In the breeding season, the male great argus pheasant clears his own patch of space on the forest floor, removing every leaf, twig, and pebble. Then he struts up and down, calling loudly to attract a female. If one arrives, he dances in front of her, spreading out his long wing feathers, which are decorated with dazzling golden eyespots.

Great hornbill
(*Buceros bicornis*)
This bird has a large, yellow casque and a loud, roaring call.

Helmeted hornbill
(*Rhinoplax vigil*)
The only species of hornbill to have a solid casque, made of a substance like ivory.

Rhinoceros hornbill
(*Buceros rhinoceros*)
Casque turns up at the end like a rhino's horn.

Rufous-necked hornbill
(*Aceros nipalensis*)
This hornbill has no casque at all.

Great argus
(*Argusianus argus*)
Length: male (including tail)
6 ft 7 in (2 m); female 2 ft 6 in (76 cm)

Nests made of saliva.

Edible-nest swiftlet
(*Aerodramus fuciphagus*)
Length: 5 in (12.5 cm)

Edible-nest swiftlet

Thousands of these swiftlets nest in caves along the coasts or in tropical rainforests. Those that live in caves use cup-shaped nests made almost entirely out of their own saliva, which hardens like cement. The nests are stuck to the walls and roofs of the caves. People collect these nests to make "bird's nest soup," so they have become valuable.

Mangrove swamps grow along the coasts and are rich in fish for birds such as storks and kingfishers to eat.

Greater Philippine Eagle · **Common Tailorbird** · **Great Argus** · **Green Broadbill** · **Blue-crowned hanging parrot** · **Edible-nest Swiftlet** · **Great Hornbill** · **Rhinoceros Hornbill** · **Rufous-necked Hornbill** · **Helmeted Hornbill**

Brilliantly colored scarlet-rumped trogons are found in forests throughout Southeast Asia. They feed mainly on fruit and large insects living among the leaves.

The male grows two long tail feathers in the breeding season.

Nest is built inside a cradle of leaves sewn together by the bird.

Long, sharp bill for making holes in leaves.

Green broadbill

The shiny green feathers of the green broadbill blend in well with the leaves of its forest home. This makes it hard for predators to spot. The broadbill moves slowly about the forests in small flocks, searching for fruits, buds, and insects. As it feeds, it often makes whistling or bubbling noises, which sound like a frog.

The male is a brighter shade of green than the female and has black wing bars and neck spot.

Common tailorbird
(*Orthotomus sutorius*)
Length: 5½ in (14 cm)

Common tailorbird

This bird gets its name from its remarkable nest, which it makes by sewing together one or more leaves on a bush or low tree branch. The tailorbird uses its bill as a needle to make a row of holes in the edges of the leaves. Then it pulls spider or insect silk, or cottony plant material, through the holes, one stitch at a time. The tailorbird builds its nest inside this "pocket" of leaves.

Green broadbill
(*Calyptomena viridis*)
Length: 7 in (17 cm)

Hanging parrot rests and sleeps upside down, with its body arched backward.

Blue-crowned hanging parrot
(*Loriculus galgulus*)
Length: 6 in (14.5 cm)

Blue-crowned hanging parrot

This sparrow-sized parrot flies through the treetops, feeding on nectar, flowers, fruits, and seeds. Like a woodpecker, it sometimes holds its tail stiffly against a branch or tree trunk to prop itself up. At night, the parrot hangs upside down from a branch like a bat. This may help it hide from predators that hunt at night.

Japan and China

MILLIONS OF PEOPLE live in crowded cities in the lowland and coastal areas of Japan and China, so there are few places left for birds to live. Some birds, such as the Okinawa rail, are close to extinction. But the mountains and forests inland remain home to many birds, especially pheasants and cranes.

The islands of Japan have been separated from mainland Asia for millions of years, and many birds have evolved into distinct Japanese species. The large variety of birds in Japan is due partly to the different habitats, but also to the climate, which ranges from warm Kyushu in the south to cold Hokkaido in the north. In China, the forests of the southwest are a refuge for birds such as Temminck's tragopan and the golden pheasant. Northern China consists of harsh deserts and grasslands, but sandgrouse and bustards survive there.

Steller's sea-eagle

The Japanese call the spectacular Steller's sea-eagle "the great eagle." Every winter, large numbers of these birds gather in the steep, wooded valleys of northeast Hokkaido. Here they are protected from the fierce winter winds at night and go out hunting for fish during the day. They swoop down to the surface of the sea to snatch fish in their powerful, curved talons. Steller's sea-eagles also feed on the carcasses of sea lions and other dead animals.

Steller's sea-eagle
(*Haliaeetus pelagicus*)
Length: 3 ft 3 in (1 m)

The male has bright red patches around his eyes.

Male mikado pheasants have long tails.

Mikado pheasant
(*Syrmaticus mikado*)
Length: male 2 ft 11 in (88 cm);
female 1 ft 9 in (53 cm)

Nest woven from pieces of grass, leaves, lichens, and moss.

Chinese penduline tit

The tiny Chinese penduline tit lives in reed marshes and nests in trees, usually willows. It builds an amazing hanging nest which looks like a woolly purse. Both male and female birds weave the nest, which takes about two weeks to finish. The female lays five to ten eggs in the nest and the young birds stay in it for two to three weeks after they hatch.

Chinese penduline tit
(*Remiz consobrinus*)
Length: 5 in (12 cm)

Pointed bill for poking into bark to find insects to eat.

Japanese white-eye
(*Zosterops japonicus*)
Length: 4½ in (11.5 cm)

Mikado pheasant

This pheasant only lives on the island of Taiwan. It feeds on berries, seeds, leaves, and insects in dense forests of oak, juniper, pine, and bamboo. In spring, the female lays about five to ten eggs, which take nearly a month to hatch into chicks.

Mandarin duck

The Mandarin duck prefers wetland habitats surrounded by dense deciduous forest. Like some other waterfowl, this duck nests in tree holes. After hatching, the nestlings have to jump down to the ground, but their light weight and soft, fluffy plumage means they manage this feat without injury.

Japanese white-eye

This white-eye lives in Japan and mainland China. It flies from tree to tree in flocks, searching for insects, seeds, buds, and fruit. In summer, the white-eye soaks up nectar from flowers with the brushlike tip of its tongue. In winter, it often visits people's yards to feed on small insects, soft fruit, and nectar.

Mandarin duck
(*Aix galericulata*)
Length: up to 1 ft 8 in
(51 cm)

The male's colorful feathers impress females during the breeding season.

48

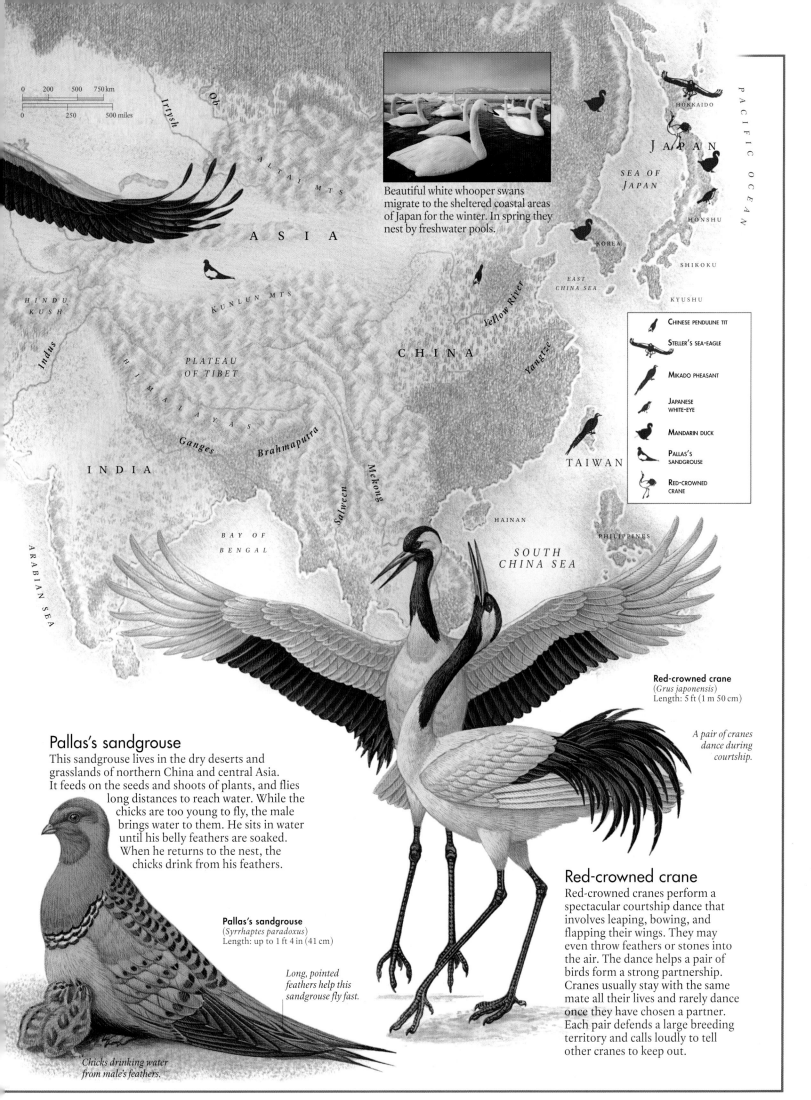

Beautiful white whooper swans migrate to the sheltered coastal areas of Japan for the winter. In spring they nest by freshwater pools.

Map labels:

0 200 500 750 km
0 250 500 miles

Irtysh · Ob · ALTAI MTS · ASIA · HINDU KUSH · Indus · KUNLUN MTS · PLATEAU OF TIBET · HIMALAYAS · Ganges · Brahmaputra · Salween · Mekong · Yellow River · Yangtze · CHINA · INDIA · BAY OF BENGAL · ARABIAN SEA · HAINAN · SOUTH CHINA SEA · PHILIPPINES · TAIWAN · EAST CHINA SEA · KOREA · SEA OF JAPAN · JAPAN · HOKKAIDO · HONSHU · SHIKOKU · KYUSHU · PACIFIC OCEAN

Legend:
- CHINESE PENDULINE TIT
- STELLER'S SEA-EAGLE
- MIKADO PHEASANT
- JAPANESE WHITE-EYE
- MANDARIN DUCK
- PALLAS'S SANDGROUSE
- RED-CROWNED CRANE

Red-crowned crane
(*Grus japonensis*)
Length: 5 ft (1 m 50 cm)

A pair of cranes dance during courtship.

Pallas's sandgrouse

This sandgrouse lives in the dry deserts and grasslands of northern China and central Asia. It feeds on the seeds and shoots of plants, and flies long distances to reach water. While the chicks are too young to fly, the male brings water to them. He sits in water until his belly feathers are soaked. When he returns to the nest, the chicks drink from his feathers.

Pallas's sandgrouse
(*Syrrhaptes paradoxus*)
Length: up to 1 ft 4 in (41 cm)

Long, pointed feathers help this sandgrouse fly fast.

Chicks drinking water from male's feathers.

Red-crowned crane

Red-crowned cranes perform a spectacular courtship dance that involves leaping, bowing, and flapping their wings. They may even throw feathers or stones into the air. The dance helps a pair of birds form a strong partnership. Cranes usually stay with the same mate all their lives and rarely dance once they have chosen a partner. Each pair defends a large breeding territory and calls loudly to tell other cranes to keep out.

AUSTRALASIA

AUSTRALASIA IS MADE UP of Australia and the islands of New Zealand and New Guinea, together with thousands of smaller Pacific islands. Australasia has been cut off from the rest of the world for millions of years, and many of the birds in the region are not found anywhere else. These include scrub-birds, lyrebirds, and the emu in Australia, bowerbirds in Australia and New Guinea, and the kiwis of New Zealand. Some birds that are common in other parts of the world are not found in Australasia, for example there are no pheasants or woodpeckers. A number of birds migrate to Australasia to escape bad weather at certain times of year—waders fly in from the north and seabirds from the south.

Since colonists arrived in Australasia about 200 years ago, many of the forests have been cleared, and the introduction of sheep, cattle, and rabbits to the ecosystem has destroyed many bird habitats.

Climate and landscape

The middle of Australia, called the outback, consists mainly of desert and has a hot, dry climate, although the southern coasts are cooler and wetter. A tropical climate, with warm, wet weather all year, occurs in northeast Australia and in New Guinea. New Zealand is cooler, with a temperate climate. The seasons in this southern part of the world are opposite to those in the north. For instance, when it is summer in Europe, it is winter in Australasia.

Australia on the move

Over millions of years, continental drift has moved Australia slowly northward. About 100 million years ago, it was attached to Antarctica. But about 50 million years ago, it split off and started to drift. For about the next 30 million years, Australia was isolated from the rest of the world and many of its unique birds evolved. By about 10 million years ago, it had drifted near enough to Asia for some Southeast Asian birds to move into northern Australia.

AMAZING BIRDS OF AUSTRALASIA

Speedy sleeper
The spine-tailed swift flies at speeds of up to 62 mph (100 kph) and can sleep while flying through the air.

Strong scent
The male musk duck has a strange pouch of skin under his bill which he uses to impress a female during his courtship display. The bird's name comes from the musky scent it produces during the breeding season.

Musk duck
(*Biziura lobata*)

Curved bill
The wrybill of New Zealand is the only bird with a bill that curves to the right.

Australian pelican
(*Pelecanus conspicillatus*)

Longest bill
The Australian pelican has the longest bill in the world. It can be up to 1 ft 7 in (47 cm) long.

Biggest nest mound
The malleefowl builds a "compost heap" to keep its eggs warm until they hatch. The nest mound can be up to more than 16 ft (5 m) wide and 3 ft 3 in (1 m) deep.

Biggest birds
The emu and cassowary are the second and third largest birds in the world, after the ostrich. Like the ostrich, emus and cassowaries are too heavy to fly.

FACTS ABOUT AUSTRALASIA

Largest rock
Uluru (also called Ayers Rock), is the world's largest free-standing rock. It lies in central Australia and is 4 miles (6 km) long and 1½ miles (2.4 km) wide. It towers 1,143 ft (348 m) high above the desert floor.

Number of birds
More than 1,700 species of bird live in Australasia. About 45 percent of the birds that breed in Australia do not occur anywhere else in the world.

Longest river
The Murray-Darling is the largest river system in Australia—it is about 2,330 miles (3,750 km) long.

Largest coral reef
The Great Barrier Reef, off the northeast coast of Australia, is the largest living structure on Earth. It stretches down the coast for over 1,243 miles (2,000 km).

Highest geyser in the region
The Pohutu geyser, in the volcanic region of New Zealand's North Island, is a violent jet of steam and water that shoots out of the ground, reaching heights of 100 ft (30 m).

Least people
Fewer people live in Australasia than any other part of the world, except Antarctica. In Australia and New Zealand, sheep and cattle outnumber people by more than 10 to 1.

Flattest continent
Australia is the flattest continent. Almost two-thirds of its land surface is only 1,000–2,000 ft (300–600 m) above sea level.

Largest lake
The largest lake in the continent is Lake Eyre in Australia. The lake is often dry, but can cover an area of 3,436 sq miles (8,900 sq km) when flooded.

The outback of Australia consists of dry grassland and desert. This is partly due to the Great Dividing Range in the east, which stops moist winds from the Pacific Ocean reaching the middle of the continent.

Typical birds

Here are just a few examples of typical birds from the most important habitats of Australasia. These range from rainforests, drier eucalyptus woodlands and grasslands, to deserts, scrubland, lakes, rivers, and swamps.

Eucalyptus woodlands

The nectar and pollen of eucalyptus trees provides food for birds such as this rainbow lorikeet and many species of honeyeater, while parrots eat the seeds.

Rainforests

There are 41 species of birds-of-paradise, such as this Raggiana. Most live in the rainforests of New Guinea and surrounding islands. Four species live in Australia.

Scrublands

Butcherbirds, such as this gray butcherbird, bell magpies, and currawongs all belong to the same family, which is found only in the scrublands of Australia and New Guinea.

Lakes and rivers

Waterbirds, such as this black swan, as well as ducks and geese, feed and nest in freshwater habitats.

Swamps

Birds such as the brolga nest in swamps, which provide shelter from predators and are a source of food such as fish. Other swamp birds include bitterns, egrets, herons, and ibises.

Islands

The brown kiwi is just one of many unique flightless birds that live only on the islands of New Zealand. They evolved at a time when there were few enemies to fly away from.

Deserts

Chats, such as this orange chat, and some parrots and pigeons manage to survive in deserts. They wander over large areas to find water and nest after rainfall, when insects start to hatch and plants grow.

Woodland, Desert, and Grassland

MOST OF AUSTRALIA HAS a dry climate. Vast areas in the middle of the continent are covered by hot desert, grassland, and scrubland, called the bush or outback. Some birds, such as chats, grasswrens, parrots, and pigeons, manage to find enough seeds and fruits to survive there, although they have to fly long distances to find water. Birds of prey can also live here by feeding on the many desert reptiles and small marsupials.

In the southeast and southwest of Australia are woodlands where a variety of eucalyptus trees grow. Here the climate is generally cooler and wetter. Marshes sometimes form during the rainy season, providing food and nesting places for ibises, pelicans, black swans, and ducks. Honeyeaters and lorikeets feed on the nectar and pollen in the eucalyptus trees and in flowering shrubs, such as grevilleas and banksias. As they feed, the birds help pollinate the flowers and spread their seeds. Birds that feed on insects also find a rich supply of food on eucalyptus trees.

Sharp, pointed bill for stabbing reptiles, such as this snake.

Laughing kookaburra
(*Dacelo novaeguineae*)
Length: 1 ft 4 in (42 cm)

Laughing kookaburra
This giant member of the kingfisher family is named after its loud hooting and chuckling call. This warns other birds to keep out of its territory. Several birds may join in the laughter, usually in the early morning or late afternoon. It sometimes comes to town and city gardens to eat the food that people leave out for it, and has also been known to raid goldfish ponds.

Western spinebill
The western spinebill uses its needle-thin, curved bill to probe for nectar in flowers. Its long bill can reach inside tube-shaped flowers or push into stiff, brushlike flowers, such as banksias. It sometimes hovers in front of flowers to drink the nectar, soaking it up with a brush at the tip of its tongue.

Western spinebill
(*Acanthorhynchus superciliosus*)
Length: 6 in (15.5 cm)

A western spinebill feeds on nectar from the flowers of a red gum, which is a kind of eucalyptus.

A male brown honeyeater feeds on a banksia flower. As honeyeaters feed, they help pollinate flowers.

Splendid fairy-wren
(*Malurus splendens*)
Length: 5 in (13.5 cm)

This bird often cocks its tail when perched on a branch.

Males have shiny, bright blue feathers in the breeding season. Females are much duller in color all year.

Splendid fairy-wren
Pairs of splendid, or banded, fairy-wrens nest in small groups, with extra birds helping feed and defend the young. The helpers may be young birds that have not yet left their parents and started to fend for themselves. They help their younger brothers and sisters survive.

0   200   400   600 km
0   200   400 miles

CORAL SEA

GREAT DIVIDING RANGE

GREAT SANDY DESERT

MACDONNELL RANGES

GIBSON DESERT

A U S T R A L I A

SIMPSON DESERT

GREAT VICTORIA DESERT

Lake Eyre

Darling

NULLARBOR PLAIN

FLINDERS RANGES

Murray

GREAT AUSTRALIAN BIGHT

SOUTHERN OCEAN

TASMAN SEA

BASS STRAIT

TASMANIA

	MALLEEFOWL		TAWNY FROGMOUTH
	LAUGHING KOOKABURRA		SPLENDID FAIRY-WREN
	WESTERN SPINEBILL		
	COMMON EMU		SUPERB LYREBIRD

Tawny frogmouth

With its speckled and streaked gray and brown feathers, the tawny frogmouth is well camouflaged, against tree bark during the day. At night, it glides down from its perch to pounce on beetles, centipedes, frogs, and mice on the woodland floor. It snaps up insects from among the fallen leaves with its huge, wide bill. The tuft of stiff feathers at the base of the bill acts like a cat's whiskers, helping the bird find its way or sense food in the dark.

Tawny frogmouth
(*Podargus strigoides*)
Length: 1 ft 9 in (53 cm)

The frogmouth looks like a dead branch when it keeps very still in this stiff, upright position.

Common emu

The emu has very small wings and cannot fly, although it can run fast on its long legs. To find enough to eat, an emu may move vast distances in a year, following the rains. It also stores food as fat in its body and survives on this in hard times. Several females lay their eggs in a hollow in the ground and the male looks after them.

Common emu
(*Dromaius novaehollandiae*)
Length: 6 ft 1 in (1 m 90 cm)
Height: 6 ft 1 in (1 m 90 cm)

The emu can run at up to 30 mph (48 kph) to escape from danger.

Common emus are related to ostriches, but they have three toes on each foot, whereas ostriches only have two.

Malleefowl

The malleefowl builds a huge nest mound of wet leaves and twigs covered with sand. The female lays her eggs in the middle of the mound. As the leaves and twigs rot, they give off heat and this keeps the eggs warm. The male keeps a constant check on the temperature by prodding it with his bill and makes sure it is always about 93°F (34°C). He piles on more sand to make the mound warmer or opens up the mound to cool it down if necessary. When the chicks hatch, they dig their own way out.

This bird is named after the male's two outer tail feathers, which are shaped like a Greek musical instrument called a lyre.

A male tests the temperature of the nest mound with his bill.

Superb lyrebird

The male superb lyrebird dances and sings on mounds of soil to attract females for mating and to drive away rival males. He fans out his long tail and arches it forward over his head to form a shimmering silvery curtain. His body is almost hidden underneath the towering tail. The female builds a nest and looks after the single egg on her own until the young bird leaves the nest at about seven weeks old.

Malleefowl
(*Leipoa ocellata*)
Length: 2 ft (60 cm)

Superb lyrebird
(*Menura novaehollandiae*)
Length: male (including tail)
up to 3 ft 3 in (1 m);
female 2 ft 8 in (80 cm)

Strong feet for digging in the sand

Long, powerful legs

Rainforests

THE BIRDS OF THE lush rainforests of northeastern Australia resemble those of New Guinea more than the rest of Australia. The two regions were joined for much of their history and have a similar warm, wet climate with rain all year. Their rainforests are rich in fruit trees for birds to feed on, but are rapidly being cleared to make way for houses, farms, dams, and mines.

New Guinea's high mountains; deep, isolated valleys; and lack of mammal predators have allowed a huge variety of birds to evolve there, including the spectacular bowerbirds and birds-of-paradise. There are also more kinds of kingfisher in New Guinea than anywhere else in the world.

Victoria crowned pigeon
(*Goura victoria*)
Length: 2 ft 5 in (74 cm)

Victoria crowned pigeon

This is one of the biggest pigeons in the world—the size of a large chicken. Despite its size, this pigeon nests up to 49 ft (15 m) high in the trees. The male Victoria crowned pigeon bows his head during his courtship display to show off his splendid crest to the female. At the same time, he spreads his tail out, fans it up and down, and makes a booming call.

These pigeons fly up into trees and perch on branches to escape danger.

BOWERBIRDS

Most male bowerbirds do not have colorful and elaborate feathers. Instead, they build "bowers"—a display shelter made out of twigs—and some decorate them with colorful objects. Females choose to mate with the males that have the best bowers, then go off to build their nests safely hidden in the forest.

Satin bowerbird
(*Ptilonorhynchus violaceus*)
Length: 1 ft 1 in (33 cm)

"Avenue" bower decorated with blue things.

MacGregor's bowerbird
(*Amblyornis macgregoriae*)
Length: 10 in (25.5 cm)

"Maypole" bower; bird has large, orange crest.

Vogelkop bowerbird
(*Amblyornis inornata*)
Length: 1 ft (30 cm)

Complex "hut" bower; bird has no crest and feathers are a dull color.

Southern cassowary

This huge cassowary is the same height and weight as a small human being. It uses the tall, horny casque on its head to push aside the tangled forest undergrowth. Its long, hairlike feathers protect its body and stop it getting scratched. The southern cassowary wanders around the rainforest searching for seeds, berries, and fruits to eat.

During courtship, the male makes booming calls, puffing out his throat to make the calls louder.

Powerful legs and long claws for defense—the cassowary cannot fly to escape enemies.

Southern cassowary
(*Casuarius casuarius*)
Length: 5 ft 7 in (1 m 70 cm)
Weight: up to 121 lb (55 kg)

Stripes on the chick help camouflage it.

Blue bird-of-paradise

To show off to a female, the male blue bird-of-paradise hangs upside down from a branch and spreads out his lacy flank plumes in a shimmering fan. His long tail streamers form arches over his body while he shivers and sways to and fro. At the same time, he makes a strange, grating call, which sounds like an electric drill. Each male displays alone in special dance trees. The females choose to mate with the male that makes the best display.

Male displaying to a female.

Blue bird-of-paradise
(Paradisornis rudolphi)
Length: 2 ft 3 in (70 cm)

Male blue bird-of-paradise when not displaying.

Eclectus parrot

Male and female eclectus parrots are such different colors that they were once thought to be different species. Both have some green feathers for camouflage in the rainforest, but the female stands out more than her mate. She is the only female parrot to be brighter than the male. Eclectus parrots roost at night in groups of up to 80 birds. By day, they travel through the treetops, searching for fruits, nuts, nectar, and leaves to eat.

The male holds his tail up during courtship displays.

King bird-of-paradise
(Cicinnurus regius)
Length: 1 ft (31 cm)
Male's tail: 5½ in (14 cm)

King bird-of-paradise

The bright red feathers of the male king bird-of-paradise contrast with the dull brown of the female. The female's colors help camouflage her while she cares for the eggs and chicks. She collects all the food she needs for herself and her chicks in the rainforest, leaving the male free for his stunning courtship displays.

Feet have a strong, viselike grip on branches.

Male

Female

Eclectus parrot
(Eclectus roratus)
Length: 1 ft 6 in (45 cm)

NEW BRITAIN

NEW GUINEA

| 0 | 250 | 500 km |
| 0 | 200 | 400 miles |

ARAFURA SEA

CORAL SEA

PACIFIC OCEAN

GULF OF CARPENTARIA

A palm cockatoo feasts on fruit from the bonda plum tree. This species is Australia's biggest parrot.

SOLOMON ISLANDS

Red-breasted pygmy-parrot

This parrot lives only on New Guinea and some of the nearby islands, where there are no woodpeckers. As it clings to tree trunks, this parrot uses its spiny tail feathers for support—just like a woodpecker. It feeds on lichens and fungi and may also eat other plants and insects.

Red-breasted pygmy-parrot
(Micropsitta bruijnii)
Length: 3½ in (9 cm)

Stiff tail used as a prop.

VOGELKOP BOWERBIRD	
SATIN BOWERBIRD	MACGREGOR'S BOWERBIRD
SOUTHERN CASSOWARY	ECLECTUS PARROT
RED-BREASTED PYGMY-PARROT	KING BIRD-OF-PARADISE
BLUE BIRD-OF-PARADISE	VICTORIA CROWNED PIGEON

GREAT SANDY DESERT

AUSTRALIA

GREAT BARRIER REEF

New Zealand

NEW ZEALAND CONSISTS mainly of two large islands—North and South Island. North Island has a warm, temperate climate with active volcanoes. South Island is colder, with glaciers, mountains, and beech forests.

New Zealand does not have a great variety of bird species. This is mainly due to its isolated position. It drifted away from the other landmasses millions of years ago as a result of continental drift. However, the few species it has are very unusual. This is because New Zealand had very few mammals when it drifted off on its own, so the birds there began to live like mammals, running about and nesting on the ground. Many birds, such as the kiwi and the takahe, stopped flying altogether because there were no mammal predators to escape from. Unfortunately, these flightless birds later became easy prey for stoats and other mammals that people introduced to the islands.

Kea
Kea
(*Nestor notabilis*)
Length: 1 ft 7 in (48 cm)

Long top bill for tearing into fruit, leaves, insects, and dead animals. The male's top bill is longer than the female's.

This unusual parrot lives in much colder habitats than most others, sometimes even in snow. In summer, it lives in the mountains but it moves down to the forests on the coast in winter. The kea is named after the sound of its call, which echoes around the steep mountainsides. Both parents take care of the young until they are ready to leave the nest after about 13 weeks.

Little penguin

The smallest penguin in the world lives around the coasts and islands of New Zealand. The little penguin, also known as the blue or fairy penguin, spends the day fishing at sea, but comes ashore at night. In the breeding season, little penguins pair up with the same mates at the same nest site year after year. They nest in a cave, among rocks or grass, or in a burrow.

Strong flippers and webbed feet for swimming fast underwater

Little penguin
(*Eudyptula minor*)
Length: 1 ft 6 in (45 cm)

Map labels
TASMAN SEA
NORTH ISLAND
PACIFIC OCEAN
BAY OF PLENTY
EAST CAPE
RAUKUMARA RANGE
Lake Taupo
KAIMANAWA RANGE
HAWKE BAY
Rangitikei
NEW ZEALAND
TASMAN MTS
COOK STRAIT
TARARUA RANGE
SOUTH ISLAND
SOUTHERN ALPS
Rakaia
CANTERBURY PLAINS
Waitaki
STEWART ISLAND

0   50   100   150 km
0   50   100 miles

Legend
SOUTHERN BROWN KIWI
WRYBILL
KAKAPO
WEKA
KEA
TUI
LITTLE PENGUIN

The bird's bill curves to the right, yet it holds its head to the left as it feeds.

Wrybill
(*Anarhynchus frontalis*)
Length: 8 in (21 cm)

Wrybill

The wrybill is named after its crooked, or wry, bill which bends to the right at the tip, although no one is quite sure why. It is a type of wading bird related to the plover. The wrybill breeds on the stones and shingle of large riverbeds on South Island from August to December. The bird and its eggs are well camouflaged among the stones. In January it migrates to North Island.

Tui

The tui is nicknamed the parson bird because the white tuft of feathers on its throat looks like the white collar worn by Christian priests or pastors. Tuis are a kind of honeyeater, and use their brush-tipped tongues to lap up nectar from flowers. They are noisy birds that fly at high speed. In the breeding season, males make spectacular dives to impress females. They roll and loop the loop as they hurtle downward.

White throat tuft bobs up and down as the bird sings. Females have smaller throat tufts than males.

Strong wings help the bird keep its balance as it walks around.

Tuis often gather in large numbers where there is a rich food supply.

Tui
(*Prosthemadera novaeseelandiae*)
Length: 1 ft 1 in (32 cm)

Weka
(*Gallirallus australis*)
Length: 2 ft (60 cm)

Powerful feet for running fast when hunting or trying to escape enemies.

Weka

The inquisitive weka cannot fly despite its well-developed wings. It feeds on all kinds of food, from grass, seeds, and fruit to mice, birds, eggs, and beetles. It even steals food from trash cans near houses. Wekas have been introduced to some of New Zealand's smaller islands and have caused serious problems. They have damaged the plants and killed off many other birds that live on the ground. They are, however, good at killing the rats that attack New Zealand's rare birds.

Kakapo
(*Strigops habroptila*)
Length: 2 ft 1 in (64 cm)

Southern brown kiwi

The Southern brown kiwi cannot fly and behaves more like a mammal than a bird. It comes out at night and stalks through bushes and leaves in the forests, sniffing out food with nostrils on the tip of its long bill—it is rare for a bird to have such a good sense of smell. The kiwi is covered in thick, shaggy feathers, so it even looks furry like a mammal. The feathers help protect it from thorny bushes.

Green feathers blend into a background of ferns and other forest plants and help camouflage the bird.

Long, thin bill for probing for food such as earthworms, insects, spiders, and berries

Southern brown kiwi
(*Apteryx australis*)
Length: 2 ft 2 in (65 cm)

Strong legs for running and powerful claws that can scratch for food

Kakapo

This is one of the rarest parrots in the world. The kakapo lives on the ground and only comes out at night. It is too heavy to fly, with a thick layer of fat under its skin that makes up about 40 percent of its body weight. In the breeding season, males gather together at special places in the forest and make loud, booming calls that carry for up to ½ mile (1 km). To make the calls louder, they dig a hollow under tree roots, which works like a megaphone. They also expand their bodies with air, like a balloon.

Antarctica

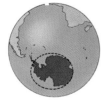

ANTARCTICA IS THE coldest and windiest place on Earth. Unlike the Arctic, which is an ocean surrounded by land, Antarctica is a huge area of land surrounded by ocean. Most of the land is covered by ice. Little rain or snow falls, so there is hardly any fresh water for birds to drink.

All birds in Antarctica are coastal. Seabirds have denser feathers than most land birds to keep them warm, and are better at flying in stormy weather. In summer, some of the ice around the coasts melts and millions of seabirds such as albatrosses, petrels, penguins, and shearwaters come ashore to lay eggs and raise their young. The Antarctic summer lasts for only about four months when it is light most of the time. During the winter, most of the birds leave Antarctica and roam widely over the southern oceans in search of food.

Kelp gulls fly slowly and often glide with their long wings stretched out.

Kelp gull

The huge kelp gull, or southern black-backed gull, is the only gull that stays in the Antarctic all year. Kelp gulls are good at catching fish, but they also eat shellfish, dead animals, and the eggs and young of other birds. They sometimes carry shellfish up into the air and drop them onto rocks to break them open. Both parents sit on the eggs for about a month to keep them warm, and the chicks can fly when they are about five to six weeks old.

Kelp gull
(*Larus dominicanus*)
Length: 2 ft 2 in (65 cm)
Wingspan: 4 ft 8 in (1 m 42 cm)

Birds grow wispy crests in the breeding season.

Jagged, hooked bill for grasping slippery fish

Imperial shag

The imperial shag has webbed feet for swimming. Its feathers soak up water, so its weight increases and it can sink and dive more easily. But it has to spread out its wings to dry after a swim. The imperial shag nests in huge colonies on sheltered coastal ledges or among rocks. The helpless young are more likely to survive where there are large numbers of adults to drive away attackers. The nest is made of a pile of seaweed, which is stuck together with the birds' droppings, called guano.

Imperial shag
(*Leucocarbo atriceps*)
Length: 2 ft 6 in (76 cm)

Huge, hooked bill for gobbling up fish or squid

During the courtship display the birds face one another, make groaning noises, snap their bills open and shut, and fence with their bills.

Large eyes for searching for food out at sea

Wandering albatross

This magnificent albatross has the largest wingspan of any bird alive today. On its long, narrow wings, it glides effortlessly over the southern oceans at great speed, using air currents rising off the waves to lift it up into the air. It comes to the Antarctic islands only to nest. The chicks stay in the nest for almost a year before they grow all their feathers for flying. The parents feed out at sea, then cough up some of this food for the chicks to eat. Both adults and young can also spray this sticky, smelly, oily food mixture up to 6 ft 2 in (2 m) to drive away predators, such as great skuas.

Wandering albatross
(*Diomedea exulans*)
Wingspan:
11 ft 6 in (3 m 50 cm)

Snowy sheathbill
Snowy sheathbill
(*Chionis albus*)
Length: 1 ft 4 in (41 cm)

Sheathbills fly well, although they spend most of their time on the ground.

Snowy sheathbill
The snowy, or pale-faced, sheathbill has a varied diet which changes with the seasons. In winter, it eats dead fish, shrimplike krill, and limpets on the shoreline. In summer, it lurks near seal and penguin colonies and feeds on seal dung, weak or injured young seals and penguins, and penguin eggs. It also picks up food scraps from the trash dumps of the many scientific bases that are in Antarctica.

Emperor penguin
(*Aptenodytes forsteri*)
Length: 3 ft 6 in (1 m 10 cm)

Emperor penguin
The enormous emperor penguin comes ashore at the start of the dark Antarctic winter and walks far inland to its nesting colonies, called rookeries. The female lays one large egg, then returns to the sea to feed. For about eight weeks, the male rests the egg on his feet and covers it with a flap of skin from his abdomen to keep it warm. During these freezing cold months, the male cannot eat and hardly moves. The female returns when the egg is due to hatch.

ANTARCTIC CIRCLE

WEDDELL SEA

ANTARCTICA

0   300   600   900 km

0   300   600 miles

ANTARCTIC PENINSULA

RONNE ICE SHELF

AMERY ICE SHELF

	KELP GULL		SNOWY SHEATHBILL
	ADÉLIE PENGUIN		EMPEROR PENGUIN
	SOUTHERN GIANT PETREL		WANDERING ALBATROSS
	IMPERIAL SHAG		

FLOOD RANGE

ROSS ICE SHELF

PRINCE ALBERT MTS

ROSS SEA

SOUTHERN OCEAN

This is a young bird. Adults are mottled gray on the head, face, and underparts.

Southern giant petrel
(*Macronectes giganteus*)
Length: 3 ft 3 in (1 m)

Southern giant petrel
Southern giant petrels or southern giant fulmars are nicknamed "stinkers" because of their unpleasant smell and because they feed on dead animals, such as seals and whales. Like vultures, they use their massive bills to rip open the bodies of dead animals. Giant petrels also kill other petrels, penguins, and albatrosses with their powerful, hooked bills.

Flippers like oars for "rowing" through the water

Adélie penguins often dive into the sea from a favorite spot. They have to keep a look out for leopard seals, which try to catch and eat them.

Adélie penguin
(*Pygoscelis adeliae*)
Length: 2 ft 4 in (71 cm)

Adélie penguin
Adélie and emperor penguins are the only two penguins that live and breed on the continent of Antarctica. In spring, Adélie penguins march inland from the sea to their rookeries. These may contain over a million birds. To mate, the birds usually return to the same rookery where they were born. They greet their mates with a special courtship display, stretching their heads and necks up, beating their wings, and making drumming and braying calls.

Travelers of the World

Every year, nearly half of all the birds in the world set off on journeys, called migration, to find food and water. Migration usually takes place at night, but some birds, such as swallows, migrate during the day. Migration journeys are often very dangerous for birds, and millions never reach their destinations. They may run out of energy or be unable to find enough food to keep going. Many migrant birds are also killed by bad weather or by people and other predators lying in wait along traditional routes.

World migration routes

This map shows the main migration routes or "flyways" that birds follow when moving from their summer breeding grounds to their winter ranges (although birds generally move over a wide area rather than a narrow path and they may switch from one flyway to another).

In North America, two-thirds of all the bird species that spend the summer there travel south for the winter. Another major winter route is from Europe to Africa. Many birds prefer to avoid crossing the Mediterranean Sea because there are no rising air currents to help them soar and glide along. So they cross it at its narrowest points—for example by the Strait of Gibraltar.

The center of huge continents, such as Asia, are good places for birds to feed and nest in spring and summer, but they get very cold in winter. So many birds migrate from the heart of Asia to the coasts.

Setting out

Before migration, birds eat as much as they can to build up fat reserves in their bodies and give them enough energy to keep going. They usually grow new feathers for the journey, too. Birds know when to migrate because of changes in the weather and also because of a biological "clock" in their brain which responds to changes in daylight hours. As the days get shorter in the fall, birds such as these barn swallows become restless, and get ready to set off by gathering in flocks.

As they migrate, the swallows feed on flying insects to keep up their strength.

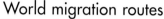

Barn swallow
(*Hirundo rustica*)

Finding the way

There is still a lot we do not understand about how birds find their way, or navigate, during migration. They seem to know instinctively which way to go because many young birds make migration journeys for the first time without the help of adults.

Birds also steer by the sun, stars, and the Earth's magnetic field. A few birds, such as shearwaters and petrels, pick up scents carried by the wind and use these to navigate their way across open oceans. Birds that migrate by day probably find their way year after year by following familiar landmarks, such as river valleys, mountain ranges, and coastlines.

Swallows have long, pointed wings for fast and powerful flight. It takes them five or six weeks to fly from Europe to Africa.

FINDING OUT ABOUT MIGRATION

To learn how far birds migrate and where they go, scientists put metal or plastic rings on their legs. The rings are numbered or color-coded and have an address on them, like the one this juvenile white-tailed eagle is wearing. It is then possible to identify individual birds and keep records of their migration movements. Another way of tracking birds' movements over shorter distances is by using a radio collar.

Common cranes migrate by day and by night from Europe to Africa.

The journey

Birds use a lot of energy for continuous flapping flight, so on long journeys they have to try and conserve their strength. Some, such as these common cranes, fly in a V-formation so that the birds following the leader do not use up as much energy pushing aside the air as they fly. Others, such as white storks, make use of rising hot air currents—called thermals—to glide and soar without using up any energy. Seabirds glide on currents rising off the ocean waves. Some birds can build up enough stores of body fat to fly nonstop for four days; others have to stop and feed every day.

Common crane
(*Grus grus*)

Birds often migrate in flocks of thousands of birds. Flying in a V-formation helps these common cranes save energy on a long journey.

Short-tailed shearwater
(*Ardenna tenuirostris*)

Migration from north to south

In the northern hemisphere, where much of the land is covered with ice and snow in winter, many birds, including the American golden plover, migrate. They spend summer in the north and fly south to warmer places for the winter, returning north again in spring.

Apart from these birds making their return journey, far fewer land birds migrate from the southern to the northern hemisphere. But several southern seabirds, such as the short-tailed shearwater, do migrate over the Equator to the oceans of the northern hemisphere for the summer because the climate is warmer and there is more food there.

American golden plover
(*Pluvialis dominica*)

This shearwater nests in Tasmania, in Australia, and on islands in the South Pacific Ocean. In April, it flies north to Japan and east to the United States, before heading south again for the winter.

The American golden plover nests in the tundra of Alaska and northern Canada and migrates down to the pampas of South America to spend the winter there.

AMAGING MIGRANTS

Arctic tern
(*Sterna paradisaea*)

Champion migrant
Every year, the Arctic tern flies from the top to the bottom of the world and back again—a distance of about 22,000 miles (36,000 km).

High fliers
Most birds fly below 300 ft (91 m) on migration, but some cross high mountains. Bar-headed geese in the Himalayas migrate at heights of more than 31,168 ft (9,500 m).

Weight-watcher
Small birds, such as the blackpoll warbler, may double their weight before migrating in order to "fuel" their journey.

Tiny migrant
Most hummingbirds do not migrate, but the ruby-throated hummingbird travels up to 2,000 miles (3,200 km) across the eastern US and the Gulf of Mexico to Central America. These tiny birds must refuel to sustain such a long flight.

Ruby-throated hummingbird
(*Archilochus colubris*)

Birds in Danger

ALL OVER THE WORLD, bird species are in danger of going extinct. When this happens, every member of a kind of bird dies and the species is lost forever. About 13 percent of birds are threatened with extinction. Over millions of years, bird species die out naturally and new ones evolve to take their place. But within the last few centuries, humans have sped up the extinction process. They increase threats to bird survival by destroying habitats, causing pollution, hunting birds, and trapping them to keep in cages. Many kinds of birds urgently need our help. Fortunately, there are people out there working to conserve birds.

Threatened birds

These are some bird species that have been endangered with extinction. Some, such as the ivory-billed woodpecker, are now probably extinct. But others, such as the St. Vincent parrot, have been saved by protection of their habitat or through captive breeding.

St. Vincent parrot
(*Amazona guildingii*)
Americas

Noisy scrubbird
(*Atrichornis clamosus*)
Australia

Chatham Island black robin
(*Petroica traversi*)
New Zealand

Gurney's pitta
(*Pitta gurneyi*)
Thailand

Eskimo curlew
(*Numenius borealis*)
Americas

Ivory-billed woodpecker
(*Campephilus principalis*)
Americas

Habitat destruction

This is the most serious threat to bird life today. Bird species are adapted to live in particular habitats, and when these habitats are destroyed, the birds that rely on them may disappear. Humans have changed bird habitats because of the ways we use the land. Forests are cleared for timber and farming, grasslands are changed into crops, wetlands are drained, and shorelines have been used for building. Some of these habitats are home to such a rich variety of species that, when they are destroyed, hundreds of bird species become threatened with extinction. Twenty percent of the Amazon rainforest is already gone. Deforestation in the Philippines has driven the Philippine eagle to the edge of extinction. In order to help protect bird species, countries around the world set aside areas of habitat that are preserved. These reserves aim to keep birds and other wildlife safe.

Greater Philippine eagle
(*Pithecophaga jefferyi*)

Asian crested ibis
(*Nipponia nippon*)

The Asian crested ibis was nearly lost to extinction because its wetland habitats—such as rice paddies—were converted to dry wheat crops, and its nesting trees were felled.

Hunting

Some species of birds are deliberately targeted by human hunters. In the 1880s, many birds, such as egrets, were killed for their showy feathers, which ended up in women's hats. Concern over species decline led to two new important bird conservation organizations: the National Audubon Society in the US and the RSPB (Royal Society for the Protection of Birds) in the UK. They helped set up new laws to protect birds, but this came too late for some. The dodo and the passenger pigeon were both ruthlessly hunted to extinction. When so many adult birds are killed in such a short space of time that they cannot breed quickly enough, the species becomes extinct. Hunting birds for food is not so common today, but many species are still killed for sport, and birds that follow the same migration routes each year are easy targets.

Great Indian bustard
(*Ardeotis nigriceps*)

People collect thousands of common murre eggs from breeding colonies off the coasts of the Faroe Islands.

Widespread hunting for food and sport has left the great Indian bustard critically endangered.

Akohekohe
(*Palmeria dolei*)

Introduced species

As people have moved from place to place, they have brought with them a variety of animals. Some, such as rats and mosquitoes, came by accident. Others, such as cats, mongooses, and stoats, were brought deliberately as pets or to control pests. But introduced animals ended up preying on local birds that had no defense against these intruders. This was a particular problem on islands, where many bird species are flightless or lived on the ground. On the Pacific islands, populations of ground-nesting seabirds have halved because of introduced rats and cats. And nearly half the songbird species on the Hawaiian Islands have been wiped out by diseases such as malaria, carried by introduced mosquitoes. Because they had never been exposed to malaria before, birds such as the Akohekohe have not developed immunity and so the disease kills them quickly. Stoats were introduced into New Zealand to try to control the rising numbers of rats and other small mammals. Unfortunately, they raided the eggs and chicks of the South Island takahe, a rare flightless bird, and it almost became extinct as a result.

Stoat
(*Mustela erminea*)

South Island takahe
(*Porphyrio hochstetteri*)

Trade in caged birds

Caged songbird

Many people like to keep birds in cages or aviaries as pets because of their beautiful colors, their songs, or their company. Birds are trapped all over the world, and this has threatened many species with extinction. Unfortunately, large numbers of birds die during capture, while waiting to be sold, or on their journey to a life in captivity. For every 10 birds caught in the wild, only about one may ever reach a pet shop. In the past, songbirds such as finches made up about 80 percent of birds traded this way—with parrots making up most of the rest. In 2005, the European Union set up a ban that reduced bird trade by a staggering 90 percent, but shifted the focus. Today, parrots make up more than three-quarters of traded bird species, with most coming from the tropical Americas and Africa.

Pollution

The activities of people and industry release harmful chemical substances into the environment, and these can threaten birds. Chemical pesticides and fertilizers used on crops, poisonous fumes released from factories, and accidental oil spills can all damage habitats and the birds that live in them. In the 1960s, it was discovered that pesticides could build up in food chains and kill top predators such as birds of prey. In much of the world, controls on pollution are now in place to help protect habitats from its effects, but birds are still being poisoned in many countries. In recent years, plastic pollution has become a major concern—especially in ocean habitats. Today, 90 percent of seabirds are accidentally eating plastic, leaving less room for their actual food. Meanwhile, global warming caused by burned fossil fuels is melting polar ice, changing polar habitats and disrupting the migration patterns of birds.

The end of the line

Some birds have died out completely. One example is the dusky seaside sparrow. Until the 1940s, thousands of these small songbirds lived in the salt marshes on the east coast of Florida, in the United States. Then in the mid-1950s, Cape Canaveral and the Kennedy Space Center Visitor Complex were built on these marshes and dykes were constructed to stop the tidal flooding. The sparrows needed the floodwaters to provide food for their survival, so they soon began to die out. Some birds were protected in a wildlife refuge, but in 1975, fire destroyed their habitat and no females have been seen since. The last dusky seaside sparrow died in 1987.

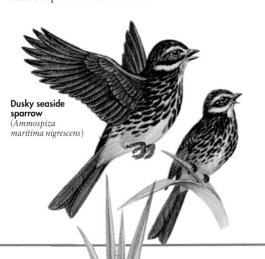

Dusky seaside sparrow
(*Ammospiza maritima nigrescens*)

WHAT WE CAN DO TO HELP

The world's rare birds need our help if they are to survive. Birds are closely linked to all the other wildlife on the planet, so if there are problems for birds, these serve as a warning of problems for plants, animals, and people. We can help by doing the following:

- Set aside areas of land and water as nature reserves or wildlife sanctuaries where birds will be protected from disturbance, hunting, and introduced species.

- Set up more artificial feeding areas for birds to help them survive in harsh climates.

- Breed rare birds in captivity and release them back into the wild. Numbers of the pink pigeon were built up in this way.

- Ban the hunting of rare species and stop birds being shot on migration.

- Stop keeping wild birds in cages and use birds bred in captivity instead.

Pink pigeon
(*Nesoenas mayeri*)

- Reduce the amount of pollution, especially from oil spills and pesticides.

- Carry out research to find out as much as possible about how birds live, so we can plan the best ways to conserve them.

- Pass international laws to protect endangered species.

- Join conservation organizations to protest, raise money, and make other people aware of the problems.

INDEX

ACKNOWLEDGMENTS

Dorling Kindersley would like to thank the following:

Rachael Foster, David Gillingwater, and Mark Thompson for design assistance; Bharti Bedi for editorial assistance; Aditya Katyal and Vagisha Pushp for picture research; Harish Aggarwal, Suhita Dharamjit, Priyanka Sharma, and Saloni Singh for the jacket; Lynn Bresler for compiling the index; and Jessica Cawthra for proofreading.

Maps Andrew MacDonald
Globes and diagrams John Hutchinson
Cartographic consultant Roger Bullen
Bird symbols Heather Blackham

The publisher would like to thank the following for their kind permission to reproduce their photographs:
(Key: a-above, b-below/bottom, c-center, f-far, l-left, r-right, t-top)

7 Getty Images: Moment / Andre Distel Photography (cla); E+ / LeoPatrizi (c). **9 Dreamstime.com:** Steven Prorak (tr). **10 Dreamstime.com:** Valio84sl (tr). **11 Alamy Stock Photo:** David Wall (tl). **Getty Images:** UIG / Don & Melinda Crawford (bl). **12 iStockphoto.com:** DonLand (c). **13 Getty Images:** RooM / Alfredo Piedrafita (tc). **15 Dreamstime.com:** Donald Fink (cra). **16 Dreamstime.com:** Kushnirov Avraham (cb). **17 Dreamstime.com:** John Anderson (ca). **19 Dreamstime.com:** Chrismrabe (bl). **20 Dreamstime.com:** Kalypsoworldphotography (br). **22 Alamy Stock Photo:** Morley Read (cr). **23 Dreamstime.com:** Filip Fuxa (cb). **25 Getty Images:** Stone / Richard I'Anson (clb). **26 Dreamstime.com:** Deborah Lee Rossiter (bc). **27 Alamy Stock Photo:** Chris Craggs (tc). **Dreamstime.com:** Jakub Barzycki (tl). **28 Alamy Stock Photo:** Peter Smith (c). **31 Dreamstime.com:** Franky (cr). **33 Dreamstime.com:** Erik Mandre (cra); John Platt (c). **35 Alamy Stock Photo:** FLPA (bl). **Dreamstime.com:** Mikhail Kokhanchikov (tl). **Getty Images:** Moment / © Vincent Boisvert, all right reserved (cl). **37 Dreamstime.com:** Natanael Alfredo Nemanita Ginting (tr). **38 Alamy Stock Photo:** Bill Gozansky (br). **39 Alamy Stock Photo:** Images of Africa Photobank / David Keith Jones (tl); Mint Images Limited / Mint Images (cb). **40 Alamy Stock Photo:** PhotoStock-Israel / Gilad Flesch (crb). **42 Dreamstime.com:** Josef Brůna (crb). **43 Dreamstime.com:** Kristianus Setyawan (ca). **Getty Images:** Moment / Boy_Anupong (tl). **45 Alamy Stock Photo:** Peter Tsai Photography (tc); Morten Svenningsen (bl). **47 Dreamstime.com:** Nuvisage (tc). **Getty Images:** Moment Open / Myron Tay (cr). **49 Dreamstime.com:** Ondřej Prosický (tc). **50 Dreamstime.com:** Mtphoto19 (bc); Pandeqiang (clb). **51 Dreamstime.com:** Julien Viry (tr). **52 Dreamstime.com:** Isonphoto (cr). **55 SuperStock:** Minden Pictures / D. Parer & E. Parer-Cook (clb). **61 Alamy Stock Photo:** Arterra Picture Library / Arndt Sven-Erik (tl). **62 Alamy Stock Photo:** amana images inc. / HIROYUKI TAKENO / a.collectionRF (bl); Arctic Images / Ragnar Th Sigurdsson (bc). **63 Alamy Stock Photo:** Nature Picture Library (ca)

All other images © Dorling Kindersley
For further information see: www.dkimages.com